T0067006

CULTURE SMART!

USA

THE ESSENTIAL GUIDE TO CUSTOMS & CULTURE

ALAN BEECHEY
AND GINA TEAGUE

KUPERARD

"The real voyage of discovery consists not in seeking new landscapes, but in having new eyes."

Adapted from Marcel Proust, *Remembrance of Things Past*.

ISBN 978 1 78702 321 5

British Library Cataloguing in Publication Data
A CIP catalogue entry for this book is available
from the British Library

First published in Great Britain
by Kuperard, an imprint of Bravo Ltd
59 Hutton Grove, London N12 8DS
Tel: +44 (0) 20 8446 2440
www.culturesmart.co.uk
Inquiries: publicity@kuperard.co.uk

Design Bobby Birchall
Printed in Turkey

The Culture Smart! series is continuing to expand.
All Culture Smart! guides are available as e-books, and many
as audio books. For further information and latest titles visit
www.culturesmart.co.uk

ALAN BEECHEY gained an M.A. in Psychology at Oxford University before embarking on a career in business communications, which took him from his hometown of London to New York City. He has worked for one of the world's largest banks, for leading human resources and communications consulting firms, and as an independent consultant. Now a dual citizen of the USA and the UK, he is also the author of the popular *Oliver Swithin* series of murder mysteries.

GINA TEAGUE is a trainer and writer on cross-cultural management, international relocation, and global career development. A native of the United Kingdom, she has lived and worked in France, Spain, Brazil, the USA, and Australia. During her sixteen years in New York, Gina gained an M.A. in Organizational Psychology and an Ed.M. in Counseling Psychology from Columbia University, developed a successful intercultural consultancy, and has written extensively on expatriate adjustment and career management.

CONTENTS

Map of the USA 7
Introduction 8
Key Facts 10

1 LAND AND PEOPLE 13

- Climate 14
- Regions 15
- A Nation of Immigrants 26
- Government 29
- The USA: A Brief History 34
- Covid-19 in America 53

2 VALUES AND ATTITUDES 57

- America—The Ideal 57
- Equality of Opportunity 58
- Individualism 59
- Self-Reliance 60
- That "Can Do" Spirit 61
- Vox Populi 63
- Egalitarianism 63
- Work Ethic 64
- Conservatism and Morality 66
- Giving Back 67
- Diversity 69
- Patriotism 70

3 CUSTOMS AND TRADITIONS 73

- Separation of Church and State 73
- Hatched, Matched, and Dispatched 77
- Holidays—What They Are and How Are They Celebrated 79

4 MAKING FRIENDS 89

- Friendship, American Style 90
- Getting to Know You 91

- Greetings   93
- Come on Over!   93

5 AT HOME   97

- America's Homes, Sweet Homes   97
- The Blended Family   101
- Growing Up in the USA   103
- Education   107
- The Daily Grind   111

6 TIME OUT   115

- Vacations   116
- Shop Till They Drop   116
- How to Pay   118
- Sports—Play Ball!   118
- Eating Out   125
- Culture   132

7 TRAVEL, HEALTH, AND SAFETY   145

- Arrival   147
- Hitting the Road   148
- Road Sense   151
- Taking Flight   152
- Riding the Rails   154
- Get on the Bus   155
- Local Public Transportation   155
- Where to Stay   156
- Health   157
- Safety and Security   158
- Batten Down the Hatches   160

8 BUSINESS BRIEFING   163

- Snapshot of the American Workplace   165
- The Bottom Line   171
- Management Style   172

- If You're Standing Still, You're Moving Backward   173
- Working as a Unit   173
- Meetings   174
- Presentations   175
- Negotiations   176
- Women in Business   178
- Business Entertaining   179

9 COMMUNICATING   181

- Linguistic Traditions   181
- Communication Style   183
- Body Language   188
- Humor   189
- The News Media   190
- Keeping in Touch   191
- Conclusion   194

Useful Apps   196
Further Reading   197
Index   198

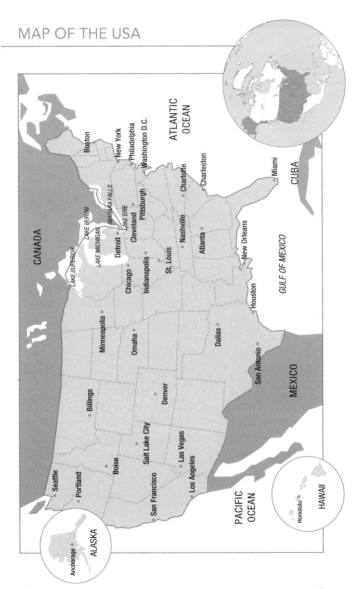

INTRODUCTION

In today's global village, who can afford not to understand the United States of America, still the world's biggest superpower, the largest economy by far, and, by many other standards, the world's most influential nation? Many facets of American life have been eagerly embraced around the world. Yet the sense of "just like in the movies" familiarity that first-time visitors often feel can be misleading. Underneath the gleaming smile of popular culture lies a varied and complex society, brimming with contrasts and contradictions. Ostentatious wealth and consumption coexist with grinding poverty, time-worn towns with vibrant cities that scrape the sky. It's a culture of go-getters, of high-tech, high achievers who invented the airplane, pioneered the Internet, put the first man on the Moon and now count Mars as their latest scientific sandbox. It's also a spiritual and compassionate country with a devotion to church and charitable works.

The sheer size and diversity of the USA can be overwhelming. How does one begin to understand a country that spans six time zones?

Culture Smart! USA provides you with a cultural "road map" to help you navigate America's human dimension. We take you on a tour of the core influences and unique ideals that have shaped American society. These deeply held values drive the behavior and attitudes you'll encounter on Main Street and in today's workplace. Ever a work in progress, the USA bears the challenge of upholding its constitutional principles at home while fulfilling its responsibility as the world's leading superpower overseas. On a lighter note, in these pages you will also get to know the Americans at work, at home, and at play.

America has an openness and generosity of spirit to newcomers. Visitors will find a dynamic, adventurous, and warm people who will accept you on your own terms. There are few cultural faux pas that can get you into trouble in this relaxed and informal society. But don't be lulled into a false sense of security. Americans hold an unshakable conviction that theirs is the best country in the world, and that while they may occasionally spare a nervous glance over their shoulder at the competition, their ultimate leadership is almost divinely assured. You'll endear yourself to your hosts by being mindful of this deep pride and of their cherished ideals.

Finally, a crucial disclaimer. In attempting to portray a nation of more than 330 million people, we can only use a very broad brush. An immigrant nation, spread across a continent that spans a sixth of the globe, newly carved from a thousand cultures, isn't going to fit a single template. Generalization is unavoidable. The rule of thumb is: be informed about cultural norms, but be flexible in applying this knowledge. In other words, when you travel to the United States, make sure you pack an open mind.

Official Name	United States of America (USA)	US or U.S. is a common alternative.
Population	333 million approx.	The world's third most populous country
Area	3,794,100 sq. miles (9,826,719 sq km) which includes the 48 contiguous states and the capital district, and the states of Hawaii and Alaska	The USA also includes various territories and dependencies, including Puerto Rico, Guam, the U.S. Virgin Islands, American Samoa, and the Northern Mariana Islands.
Capital City	Washington, D.C.	D.C. stands for District of Columbia.
Major Cities by Population	New York, Los Angeles, Chicago, Houston, Phoenix	
Terrain	Mountains in the west, vast plain across central states, hills and low mountains in the east	
Climate	Continental, with extremes of temperature and precipitation	
Currency	US Dollar	
Language	American English	The USA has no "official" language, and many government and commercial services are also provided in Spanish and Chinese.
Ethnic Makeup	White or European 76.3%; Black or African-American 13.4%; Asian 5.9%; American Indian, Alaska Native, Native Hawaiian, and other Pacific Islander 1.5%; other or mixed 2.8%. Based on 2020 Census categories, 18.5% of the population is "Hispanic" or "Latino," which is not a racial category.	

Life Expectancy	Total population 79; Male 76; Female 81
Age Structure	0–14 years 18.37%; 15–64 years 65%; 65 years or older 16.63%
Religion	Protestant (including Southern Baptist, Methodist, Lutheran, Presbyterian, and Episcopalian) 46.6%; Roman Catholic 20.8%; Mormon 1.6%; other Christian 1.7%; Jewish 1.9%; Buddhist 0.7%; Muslim 0.9%; Hindu 0.7%; other faiths 1.8%; atheist, agnostic, or none 22.8%
Government	Federal government of 50 states and the District of Columbia. The seat of government is Washington, D.C. The executive is headed by the president. The bicameral legislative body (Congress) comprises the Senate and the House of Representatives.
Economy	Free market economy for consumer goods and business services, with some government regulations.
Resources	Mineral, energy, and forest, including oil, coal, and gas.
Telephone	Country code: 1 / To dial out for international calls: 011
Time Zones	There are four times zones across the American continent. Alaska and Hawaii cover two more. Eastern: UTC minus 5 hours; Central: UTC minus 6 hours; Mountain: UTC minus 7 hours; Pacific: UTC minus 8 hours; Alaska: UTC minus 9 hours; Hawaii: UTC minus 11 hours
Media	The leading network television channels are ABC, CBS, Fox, and NBC. / There are more than 15,500 FM and AM radio stations, and 1,260 daily newspapers. Spotify and Apple Music are the leading music streaming services.

CHAPTER ONE

LAND & PEOPLE

Fifty states make up the United States of America. The "lower forty-eight," plus the District of Columbia—the 68 square miles (176 sq. km) around Washington, D.C., the nation's capital—stretch from "sea to shining sea" in a central band across the North American continent, with Canada to the north and Mexico to the south.

The other two stars on the national flag represent the states of Alaska, northwest of Canada, and Hawaii, situated in the Central Pacific, 2,500 miles (4,023 km) to the west of California. Other territories and dependencies include American Samoa, Guam, and the Northern Mariana Islands in the Pacific, and Puerto Rico and the US Virgin Islands in the Caribbean Sea.

With a landmass of nearly 3.8 million square miles (9.8 million sq. km), America is the third-largest country in the world. It has a coast-to-coast span of some 2,700 miles (4,345 km) and is as geographically diverse as it is vast, encompassing mountain ranges and endless prairie, swampy wetlands, lush rain forests, shimmering deserts, and glacial lakes. The five Great Lakes that create vast inland seas on the border between the USA and Canada form the largest body of freshwater in the world. The Missouri–Mississippi River system is the longest in North America, giving two states their names. Immortalized in the nineteenth-century writings of Mark Twain, the Mississippi was at one time the country's lifeline, connecting the upper Plains states and the South.

There are 326 Indian reservations in the United States, governed by Native American tribal nations, covering about 2.3 percent of the country's landmass.

CLIMATE

The range of altitudes together with the sheer size of the landmass produces great variations in temperature and precipitation. In a nation that is subarctic at its highest elevations and tropical at its southernmost points, temperatures can vary from below zero in the Great Lakes region to a balmy 80 degrees in Florida. On the same day!

The continental climate of the central portion of the country produces extreme conditions throughout the year. Temperatures in the Great Plains state of North Dakota have ranged between a summer high record of 121°F (49°C) and a winter low of -60°F (-51°C). With no high elevations to protect it, the interior lowlands are at the mercy of both the warm southern Gulf Stream and blasts of arctic air from the north. At times, these incompatible weather systems collide violently. Displays of nature at her most ferocious can be witnessed in the form of blizzards, hailstorms, tornadoes, and dust storms. Every year, with tragic consequences, the central plains between the Rockies and the Appalachians earn their nickname "Tornado Alley."

The western mountain states enjoy mild summers, but the higher elevations are blanketed in snow throughout the winter months. The low, desert areas of Arizona and New Mexico experience hot, dry air, although winters can be surprisingly cold.

The coastal areas are more temperate, blocked from extending their moderate influence inland by the Appalachian Mountains in the east and the Pacific Coast ranges in the west. The Gulf Stream, a warm ocean current that flows from the Gulf of Mexico northeast across the Atlantic, produces hot, wet, energy-sapping conditions for Florida and the other Gulf Coast states.

Temperatures are moderate year round on the Pacific Coast, although they start to dip as you venture northward into America's wettest region. The Cascade Range acts as a climatic divide, with the lush western side receiving up to twenty times more precipitation than the dusty plains to their east. Rising temperatures and drought conditions have brought an increase in wildfires across the western half of the country, often sparked by lightning.

REGIONS

America's malls and main streets may be taking on a uniform blandness, but there are still rich, diverse cultures to be found at the regional level. People express their regional identity in many ways, not least through the state motto on their license plates.

New England
(Maine, New Hampshire, Vermont, Massachusetts, Connecticut, and Rhode Island)

For such a small region, New England has played a disproportionate role in the country's political and cultural development. The town meetings held by church congregations to voice opinions and effect change on local issues, for example, provided the model for democratic popular government in America. The religious principles, political activism, and industriousness that shaped its history translate today into a culture characterized by community involvement and a strong work ethic.

Many of the first European settlers were English Protestants, seeking religious freedom. The area was also a crucible for anticolonialist sentiment, providing the setting for the Boston Tea Party and many of the battles of the ensuing Revolutionary War. Family fortunes amassed in Boston through fishing and shipbuilding financed the Industrial Revolution in the nineteenth century. The region's wealth established it as the intellectual and cultural center of the fledgling country.

Today, New England's whaling and manufacturing have been replaced by high-tech industries. However, its history is still evident through the Bostonian accent and the colonial-style houses and white-spired churches. The region is favored by tourists for its rugged coastline and

Boston city skyline, Massachusetts, New England.

Cape Cod's sandy beaches. Vermont's Green Mountains are home to moose and black bear.

The Middle Atlantic
(New York, New Jersey, Pennsylvania, Delaware, and Maryland)

The Mid-Atlantic region has taken center stage for much of the nation's historical and economic activity. Home to New York City's Ellis Island, the point of entry for immigrants, the region was the original melting pot into which ambitious newcomers eagerly dived. Today, there are still eight times as many people per square mile in the Northeast than there are in the West. New England's money may have financed the Industrial Revolution, but it was New Jersey and Pennsylvania's manpower that stoked the chimneys. New York replaced Boston as the financial capital, and the "Big Apple's" energy, pace, and intensity fuels and defines American capitalism. Historic

Spread over 1,317 square miles (3,411 sq. km), New York's Central Park attracts an estimated 40 million visitors every year.

Philadelphia—one of the eight cities to be declared the capital of the USA before Washington was purpose built—provided the backdrop for the Declaration of Independence (1776) and the drafting of the US Constitution.

The original farmers and traders of the region were blessed with rich farmlands, vital waterways, and forests teeming with wildlife, timber, and mineral resources. Humanity has encroached on and altered this part of the American landscape more than any other, yet it retains a stunning array of scenic landscapes. The indented coastline has rolling sand dunes and bustling harbor resorts. The lowlands of the Atlantic coastal plain incorporate both the eastern corridor of major metropolises and gently undulating farmlands. Further inland, the plains bump up against New York's Catskills and Pennsylvania's Allegheny Mountains. These subsidiary ranges are part of the Appalachian Mountain range, which forms an almost unbroken spine running parallel to the East Coast from northern Maine south to Georgia. The region's waterways are no less impressive. While it may be surrounded by motels and commercial kitsch, the sheer power of Niagara Falls, one of the world's seven natural wonders, is still breathtaking.

The Midwest
(Ohio, Michigan, Indiana, Wisconsin, Illinois, Minnesota, Iowa, parts of Missouri, North Dakota, South Dakota, Nebraska, Kansas, and Eastern Colorado)

An agricultural powerhouse of patchwork farms giving way to rolling wheat fields, the northeast corner of America's vast interior plain has long been regarded as the breadbasket of the United States. The rich soil and the landscapes first beckoned European immigrants to farm the interior plains of America. Illinois, home to the third-largest city, Chicago, attracted Poles, Germans, and Irish. Scandinavians favored Minnesota, with its familiar forests of birch and pine. Milwaukee is renowned for its European-style taverns and beer festivals.

As western settlement pushed past the Mississippi, the Midwest was transformed from an outpost into a trading and transportation hub. Spilling across the country from New York toward Chicago, a region dubbed "The Rust Belt" embraced many cities known for large-scale manufacturing, from the processing of raw materials to the production of heavy goods for industry and consumers. Detroit in Michigan, known as "Motor City" (or "Motown" to fans of R&B), is the home of the US automobile industry, which—like much traditional US manufacturing—has not had an easy ride in recent years.

This interior region is also called the "heartland," a reference to the wholesome values and unpretentious nature of its people, deemed to be representative of the nation in general. Further west, the Dakotas area is rich in both human and paleontological history, featuring Oligocene fossil beds dating back 35 million years. However, the desolate landscape evokes images of the more recent past, when the Black Hills and Badlands region formed the backdrop for battles between US soldiers, land-hungry settlers, and Native American tribes. The constant struggle against extreme weather and dust-bowl conditions has forged a stoic and taciturn nature. On its western edges, the flat prairie land of the Great Plains rises majestically to form the Rockies.

Dusk in downtown Cleveland, Ohio.

Yosemite Valley, California.

The West

(Colorado, Wyoming, Montana, Utah, California, Nevada, Idaho, Oregon, Washington)

The Rocky Mountains bisect the western portion of the continent, stretching from Montana in the north to New Mexico in the south. Moving west, the glacial basins and plains of the Intermontane Plateau include Utah's Salt Lake City, Arizona's Grand Canyon, and California's forbidding Mojave Desert. Closer to the Pacific coast, the Sierra Nevada range runs up through California. Continuing the line through the Pacific Northwest states of Oregon and Washington, the volcanic peaks of the Cascade Mountains extend to the Canadian border.

In America's western states, the forces of nature seem to have conspired to ward off visitors. Here, the mountain peaks are higher, the deserts deadlier, and the foaming river rapids swifter than anywhere else, and wildfires have become more frequent. Even the wildlife is not for the fainthearted— grizzly bears, mountain lions, and rattlesnakes call this region home. Further natural barriers have been thrown up relatively recently. In 1906, Point Reyes was at the epicenter of what became known as the San Francisco earthquake, with the infamous San Andreas Fault creating a peninsula that juts ten miles into the Pacific.

California is equally popular for the attractions of its cities—Los Angeles and San Francisco, for example—and its stunning natural beauty. Fun-loving, energetic Californians brag they have world-class ski slopes, lush vineyards, and endless beaches all in their backyard. The state has the nation's most important and diversified agricultural economy, and its sunshine and variety of landscapes also drew the motion picture industry across the continent to the West Coast.

Newcomers have long been attracted here for its sense of space, easygoing nature, and tolerance of alternative lifestyles. These days, however, they're increasingly likely to pass long-time residents heading out of the state in search of a lower cost of living.

The Southwest
(Western Texas, parts of Oklahoma, New Mexico, Arizona, Nevada, and the southern interior part of California)

The desert vistas of the Southwest have a deeply spiritual quality. Arizona's largest city, Phoenix, was so named in 1867 by Darrell Duppa because he thought the desert oasis had sprung from the ashes of an ancient civilization. Actually, Duppa's fertile "oasis" was due to a primitive but effective irrigation project, established centuries before the Europeans' arrival. Other vestiges of ancient civilizations remain in the form of the ninth-century ruins of the scientifically advanced Chaco culture and the mysterious cliff dwellings of the thirteenth-century Mogollon tribe. Mexican Pueblo settlements of sunbaked adobe structures and the abandoned communities of silver miners and gold prospectors are further reminders of the cultural diversity of the region.

Navajos believe that they have journeyed through several other worlds to this life and have always considered the land in the Southwest to be sacred. Many descendants of local tribes now live on reservations, which occupy half of these states' lands. These areas—like many others all across the USA—are called "nations," and they give a degree of self-government and autonomy to the tribe. Visitors should note that rules of conduct may change when you step onto tribal lands.

A view of Lower Monument Valley from Hunts Mesa, Navajo County, Arizona.

A reliable water supply has transformed the once desolate, forbidding desert into an attractive option for transplanted telecommuters, immigrants, and retirees. Indeed, the dry air, endless sunshine, and world-class golf courses have placed Phoenix, Albuquerque, and Tucson among the country's fastest-growing communities.

Billions of years of evolution, severe wind and water erosion, and geographical anomalies reveal themselves in dramatic fashion in some of the area's natural features. The rainbow-striped rock of the Painted Desert, the red sandstone monoliths of Monument Valley, the orange-hued Grand Canyon, and the bleached landscape of White Sands Monument all give lie to the idea that desert vistas only come in monotonous tones of brown.

The South
(Virginia, West Virginia, Kentucky, Tennessee, North Carolina, South Carolina, Florida, Georgia, Alabama, Mississippi, Central Texas, Arkansas, Louisiana, and parts of Missouri and Oklahoma)

Forged by its history, climate, and location and expressed in music, food, and the drawl of its accent, the South possesses perhaps the strongest regional personality. From the Civil War to the civil rights movement, from huge territorial acquisitions to the constant stream of immigrants, the South has been shaped by its diversity, its turbulent past, and the ongoing challenge of social integration. The conflicts—both physical and political—have created a fiercely independent spirit. While Texas is characterized as having a devil-may-care nature, the

South in general is known for its hospitality, charm, and gentle pace. The unofficial motto of the Lone Star state—"Don't mess with Texas"—reminds us that this state was once an independent nation, and still considers itself to be a republic!

The old Mason-Dixon line, which demarcated north from south in the late 1700s, may have been erased from the maps, but a strong divide still exists, as witnessed by the tenacity of the confederate flag, despite the South's defeat in the Civil War by the anti-slavery North. Both South Carolina and Mississippi passed legislation to remove the "Stars and Bars" from state grounds because of its racist association. Statues of confederate leaders are disappearing from public plinths for the same reason.

This broad sweep of states is a study in contrasts and superlatives. The ostentatious affluence of such cities as Charleston and Atlanta contrasts sharply with Mississippi shantytowns and West Virginia trailer parks. The region embraces the highlands of Missouri's Ozarks, Virginia's Blue Ridge Mountains, and Tennessee's Great Smoky Mountains, as well as the fertile cotton belt of the interior plain. A scattering of hurricane-weary coastal islands dots the lower eastern seaboard. The delicate ecosystem of the Florida Everglades sustains the sly alligator and the odd-looking manatee (fortunately "quite devoid of vanity," as the great American poet Ogden Nash once famously rhymed). Among the most evocative images of the South are the mangrove swamps and the Spanish moss dripping from ancient oaks in Louisiana bayou country.

Alaska and Hawaii

Adding to the nation's geographical diversity are the glacial mountains of Alaska, featuring America's highest peak, Mount McKinley.

A tourist's paradise, the Hawaiian Islands boast volcanic formations, tropical vegetation, the occasional black sand beach, and the highest cost of living.

A NATION OF IMMIGRANTS

"E Pluribus Unum" ("Out of many, one")
America's First National Motto

For the English seeking religious freedom, Jews fleeing pogroms in Eastern Europe, and Irish escaping famine, America represented a land of refuge and opportunity. Since 1886, the Statue of Liberty provided the first glimpse of America and a symbol of hope for the millions of immigrants who arrived in New York harbor.

The museum on neighboring Ellis Island, the site of what was once America's busiest immigration-processing center, chronicles the experiences, hardships, and eventual settlement patterns of America's newcomers. Today, nearly half of all Americans are descendants of the twelve million people, most of them Europeans, who entered the USA through Ellis Island between its peak years of 1892 and 1954.

America's ethnic tapestry has always been a work in progress. According to the 2020 Census, the US population is currently composed of 1.5 percent Native American

New arrivals wait to be processed on Ellis Island.

Indians, Alaskans, and Hawaiians, 13.4 percent "Black or African-American," and 5.9 percent Asian. Those identifying themselves as "White or European" amount to 76.3 percent. About 18.5 percent of the population is of Hispanic or Latino origin (the census uses the terms interchangeably), which is not a racial designation. Hispanic Americans may be white, black, or Asian, although many used the "other" box in the census.

While whites are distributed throughout the country, minorities tend to be more geographically concentrated. African-Americans live largely in the South and in the cities of the industrial Midwest and Northeast. Not surprisingly, Hispanic Americans are heavily concentrated in the southern border states (accounting for nearly 96 percent of the population of Laredo, Texas, for example). The Asian community, one of the fastest-growing demographics, has, for the most part, settled closer to their ports of entry on the West Coast.

Currently, the national birthrate is in negative territory and on a long-term downward trend, although there are regional variations. An aging population coupled with a dwindling Social Security fund is a matter of concern for America's politicians and employers alike. However, immigration continues to boost the population by about a million every year, and most legal immigrants go on to take American citizenship. Hispanics are faster growing as a demographic group than non-Hispanics. Illegal immigrants make up about a quarter of all immigrants and pose a variety of social, political, and economic challenges.

Births to "minorities" (that is, non-whites) already outnumber births to whites, and if current patterns continue, the white population will drop below 50 percent before the year 2045 (with the projected US population being 390 million out of a world population of nearly 9.5 billion people).

Visitors to an immigrant community are likely to see individuals adept at navigating two cultural worlds. By day, people from diverse backgrounds operate harmoniously in mainstream American society. At day's end, however, they may return home and revert to their own language, traditions, and cultural identity.

The Melting Pot

An early mention of the melting pot philosophy appears in Israel Zangwill's 1908 play, *The Melting Pot*: "Germans, Frenchmen, Irishmen, Englishmen, Jews and Russians . . . into the crucible with you all! God is making the American!"

For today's population, a "salad bowl" is a better metaphor than a melting pot. Americans often boast of the patchwork makeup of their family trees—generally Zangwill's European mix plus a little Scandinavian—but intermarriage across certain ethnic or racial lines is relatively recent.

Like a kaleidoscope, as immigrants from an increasingly wide range of countries enter the picture, the pattern of American society continues to change, struggling to balance the nation's historic values with the opportunities and challenges brought about by multiculturalism. "Can't we all just get along?" pleaded the late Rodney King famously in 1991 after an explosion of racial violence in Los Angeles. Perhaps because of America's founding principles of inclusion and diversity, they do get along for much of the time.

GOVERNMENT

The United States' system of government was established in 1789, based on the world's first written constitution (1787). The Constitution designed a system of checks and balances that would protect Americans against excessive central power. It separated the government into three branches—executive, legislative, and judicial—and balanced power between the federal government and the individual states.

A Bill of Rights (which added the first ten amendments to the Constitution in 1791) protects individual liberties from the long arm of government. Considered one of the cornerstones of American democracy, it includes the right to free speech, the right to bear arms, and the right not to incriminate oneself. It's significant that there are only two items in the Constitution that have ever placed restrictions on citizens, as opposed to government: the thirteenth amendment of 1865 took away the "right" to own slaves (but, of course, awarded the right not to be a slave); and the eighteenth amendment of 1919 brought in Prohibition. This is also the only amendment to have been repealed.

The ever-shifting distribution of powers between the different branches of government is a constant source of controversy. Applying the sometimes ambiguous words of a document written more than two centuries ago to today's societal challenges provides job security for constitutional scholars and Supreme Court justices alike. Yet few would dispute that the Constitution is remarkable in having articulated the values and aspirations of successive generations of Americans since 1787.

The Executive

The executive branch of government consists of a president and a vice president (who are elected "on the same ticket" for four years), and a cabinet composed of the heads (or secretaries) of the fifteen executive departments. The cabinet is unelected; its members, who don't have to be politicians, are appointed by the president, but require Senate approval. The president serves as head of state and commander-in-chief of the armed forces and is restricted to a maximum of two elected terms in office, not necessarily consecutive.

Capitol Hill, Washington. Home to the domed United States Capitol, the Senate, the House of Representatives, and the Supreme Court.

The Legislature

Congress, the legislative branch of government, comprises the hundred-member Senate, and the 435-member House of Representatives. The number of congressmen and women elected to the House of Representatives from each state is based on its population. Members serve two-year terms. In the Senate, each state is represented by two members. Senators serve six-year terms, with one-third of the seats being up for election every two years.

The Judiciary

The judiciary is headed by the Supreme Court of nine judges, who are appointed for life by the president. The highest court in the land, it is the final arbiter in determining the constitutionality of legislative and executive actions and maintaining the balance between state and federal institutions.

The States

With the passage of time, the delicate balance of power

has shifted away from the states, as the role of central government has steadily expanded. The individual states still retain significant administrative and policy-making autonomy, however. The visitor can be baffled by the wide variance in state laws, with everything from drinking age to abortions and capital punishment being adjudicated by geography. Most states replicate the federal structure, each having its own constitution, a chief executive (the governor), a bicameral state congress, and a judiciary.

Political Parties

The "winner take all" electoral structure favors a two-party system. Democrats tend to be more liberal than Republicans and believe in a stronger role for government. They tolerate higher taxes to pay for social programs, with the heavier tax burden falling on those with the highest income. Regarded as "the party of the people," it has particular appeal to ethnic minorities and women.

Considered to be more socially conservative and pro free enterprise than the Democrats, the Republican Party—often called the "G.O.P.," which stands for Grand Old Party—favors state rights, low taxation, with tax breaks for the wealthy, small government, and a strong military. Republicans count on a following among the middle class, business interests, and the farming community.

The liberal-versus-conservative spectrum is broad, but overall, it's well to the right of, say, European politics. (Ian Hislop, editor of Britain's satirical *Private Eye* magazine, once observed that America has "a conservative party and a very conservative party.") Communism was, of course, the antithesis of America's freedoms, but even "socialist" and "liberal"—and these days "woke"—have been hurled as insults at Democrats, while the extreme right wing often takes pride in its "know-nothing" anti-intellectualism: in 2022 some Republican Senate candidates proclaimed that they didn't believe in evolution. Divisive, "hot button" items sure to surface during campaigns still include gun control, abortion, gender identity and same-sex marriage, and even contraception and basic voting rights. A significant feature of the political scene is the well-funded special interest groups that lobby politicians to influence their policy decisions.

For most of the century, each party has counted on a devoted "base" of about 40 percent of the electorate, although its geographical location has shifted with each generation. Presidential elections are therefore decided by a fluid middle ground of independents and uncommitted voters. No president in history has ever persuaded more than 62 percent of the voting public to choose him! Third parties, such as the Greens, find it hard to make an inroad in this system.

Because of the Electoral College, the voting tendencies of the nation are analyzed on a state-by-state basis. Democratic states are labeled as blue states and Republican states are referred to as red. Currently, the blue states tend to be those lining the West Coast, clustered around the Great Lakes, or stretching north along the Eastern seaboard from Washington D.C. up to Maine. Red states sit in the center of the country.

In recent years, the divide between the two parties has been marked and increasingly vocal, and "bipartisanship" has been limited, often leading to governmental gridlock.

The Federal Electoral System

Presidential elections are held every four years, on the first Tuesday in November. The inauguration of the winning candidate is held on the following January 20.

Technically the president isn't elected by universal suffrage but by a 538-member Electoral College, which is confusing to many outsiders. Each state has a number of Electoral College votes, generally proportionate to the size of its population, but slightly favoring the smaller states. When people vote for a presidential candidate, they're actually instructing their state Electoral College to cast their votes for that candidate. In most states, the candidate who receives the most votes is awarded that state's entire allocation of Electoral-College votes. Only Maine and Nebraska divide their votes proportionally. The presidency is awarded to the candidate who receives at least 270 of the nation's 538 Electoral-College votes.

Five times in history, the College elected a presidential candidate who hadn't won the nation's popular vote: John Quincy Adams (1824), Rutherford B. Hayes (1876), Benjamin Harrison (1888), George W. Bush (1970), and Donald Trump (2016).

THE USA: A BRIEF HISTORY

Despite the presence of indigenous Amerindian tribes and evidence of a tenth-century Viking settlement in Newfoundland, the official title of "discoverer of America" is generally conferred upon the Italian explorer

Christopher Columbus, or "Cristobal Colon," as he was known to his Spanish sponsors. In one of the most profitable navigational mistakes in history, in 1492 Columbus mistook the Caribbean islands for the spice-rich East Indies, and its native people for "Indians." He made three further voyages, but never laid eyes on the North American mainland. In recent years, because of his brutality toward indigenous people, his reputation has been re-evaluated, and many public monuments have been removed. The "Columbus Day" federal holiday in October is increasingly referred to as "Indigenous People's Day."

As tales of spectacular abundance reached the shores of Europe, the race to colonize the New World got under way. The Spanish claimed large tracts of the South and Southwest. The French focused on fur trading further north. Interestingly, most of the land on the eastern seaboard, today's most populous region, was considered to be mosquito-ridden and uninhabitable. An entire island colony (Roanoke) established by Walter Raleigh off the Carolinas mysteriously disappeared. British luck changed when tobacco became Europe's new addiction. A colony was founded at Jamestown in 1607 to produce the cash crop for the British Crown. By the mid-1700s, British settlers had established thirteen colonies on the East Coast stretching from Maine to Georgia.

A Model Society

One of these was Plymouth Colony in modern-day Massachusetts, founded by the Puritan passengers of the Mayflower. The Puritans were a fundamentalist Protestant

Puritans and Native Americans depicted in *Thanksgiving at Plymouth* by American painter Jennie Brownscombe.

sect that had fled persecution by the Church of England. Their later leader, John Winthrop, envisioned their self-governing community as a "model society" in a new land. From the Puritans, America inherited the ideal that this great experiment in nation building was to be a "shining city upon a hill" for other countries to look up to.

Competing European ambitions in the new country led to the Seven Years' War (1757–63), giving Great Britain sovereignty over Canada and all of North America east of the Mississippi. Victorious but smarting from the expense of maintaining its colonies, the English authorities decided to raise American taxes. In response, the colonists united behind a banner of "No Taxation without Representation" and in 1773, knowing just how to upset the British, dumped consignments of unfairly taxed tea into Boston Harbor.

Revolution and Independence

Anti-tax protests escalated and tensions mounted, but the first shots weren't fired until April 19, 1775, when British soldiers confronted colonial rebels in Lexington, Massachusetts, and the American Revolution was under way.

On July 4, 1776, the leaders of the thirteen colonies, finally united by a common cause, approved a Declaration of Independence—it was actually signed two days later—providing for self-determination.

Some loyalists kept their allegiance to the British Crown, but the other colonists, with clandestine support from France, Spain, and the Dutch Republic, quickly gained control of the country. A British naval landing in New York brought the conflict to a standoff, but a failed invasion from Canada in 1777 led to a major defeat for the British at Saratoga, persuading the French to support the revolution openly. A second significant defeat and surrender for the British at Yorktown, Virginia, in 1781 signaled the final victory of the new Americans and their European allies, although fighting continued until the signing of the Treaty of Paris two years later, which created an independent nation.

Birth of a Nation

The "Articles of Confederation," the wartime manifesto drafted to unite the colonies, was deemed inadequate to address the post-Revolution challenges of governing the country. Summoned to Philadelphia in 1787 to

Washington Crossing the Delaware by Emanuel Leutze.

revise it, the state delegates (later immortalized as the nation's "Founding Fathers") preferred to start with a blank slate—a metaphor for the newly independent country. The result was the US Constitution, a document that has provided the political and legal framework for the country since its ratification in 1788. The following year, George Washington, Commander of the Continental Army during the Revolutionary War, became the first US president.

Manifest Destiny

Having rid itself of colonial overlords, America turned its attention westward. In 1803 President Thomas Jefferson purchased the Louisiana Territory from the cash-strapped Napoleon. This three-cents-per-acre bargain doubled the country's size, pushed the boundaries as far west as the

Rockies, and gave access to the Mississippi waterway. By mid-century, a series of territorial wars and land treaties had added the present-day states of Oregon, Washington, Texas, New Mexico, Arizona, California, Utah, and Colorado to the union.

Americans believed it was their "manifest destiny" to settle all parts of North America. However, as an increasing number of settlers, gold prospectors, and cattle drivers pushed west, the fate of the Native Americans, who had long inhabited the lands, was manifestly sealed. Throughout the 1800s, Native Americans were dispossessed of their land through a series of spurious land deals, government deceptions, and bloody conflicts. The Indian Removal Act (1830) forcibly relocated tribes from their southeastern homelands to designated "Indian Territory" in Oklahoma. The route traveled and the journey itself was evocatively immortalized as the "Trail of Tears."

Hunkpapa Lakota (Sioux) leader, Sitting Bull. A revered warrior, he took part in the Battle of Little Big Horn.

THE NATIVE AMERICANS

Territorial wars, disease, and confinement to government reservations reduced the Native American population from an estimated 4.5 million at the onset of European colonization to 350,000 by 1920.

Today, after several missteps, government, society—even Hollywood—acknowledge the wrongs perpetuated in the rush to settle America. Unemployment, illiteracy, and poverty remain challenges among Native Americans. Yet they have demonstrated a great resilience of spirit: in the 2020 Census, 9.7 million people identified as Native American or Alaskan Native—alone or in combination with another race. Most of these people don't live on tribal lands. Many Native Americans have made unique contributions to American society while continuing to honor their cultural heritage. In 2021, President Joe Biden appointed Deb Haaland as his Secretary of the Interior, the first Native American to serve in a cabinet position. (Using the generic term "Indian" for a Native American is acceptable.)

Visitors to the Southwest or Plains states can best learn about the Native American culture and way of life by listening, observing—and leaving the cameras at home.

Later, the influx of settlers attracted to free government land by the Homestead Act (1862) sparked clashes with the Great Plains tribes. Called in to protect the new farming settlements, the US army fought a series of wars with the Cheyenne, Arapaho, and Sioux between 1862 and 1876. The battles included the last US military defeat on American soil, when Custer's "last stand" was overrun by the Sioux at Little Big Horn. Today, a mountain-sized monument to Chief Crazy Horse, in South Dakota, still under construction since 1948, recognizes him as a symbol of the resistance and heartbreak of the Indian nations.

The Civil War

The "peculiar institution" of slavery started in the early 1600s, when Africans were forcibly transported to the United States and sold at auction to replace poor whites and Native Americans as "indentured servants." As the agricultural economy developed in the South, between 1619 and 1865, three million slaves were brought to the United States to labor on Southern tobacco, sugar cane, and cotton plantations.

Slavery drove a deep wedge into the existing political and economic divisions between the North and South. The farms and industries of the populous Northern states had less need for slaves and abolished the practice in 1804. Congress outlawed the import of slaves into the USA after 1808, but individual states could determine their own policies on the continued trading and "employment" of slaves. As, one by one, newly admitted

Photographic portrait of President Abraham Lincoln, 1863.

western states chose to join the North in becoming "free states," the South felt the political and economic tide shifting against them.

In opposing slavery, the North claimed the moral high ground. The South countered that the very fabric of its economy and society was at stake. When antislavery crusader Abraham Lincoln was elected president (1860), the Southern states defiantly announced they were seceding from the union and forming a Confederacy.

The four-year Civil War (1861–65) that followed was an uneven contest. The industrial North had the advantage in manpower, sophisticated communications, and manufacturing infrastructure. The agrarian South had fine military leaders and a steely resolve, but defeated by Sherman's victory in Atlanta (1864) and subsequent march across the South, the Confederate states surrendered in 1865. Slavery was formally abolished throughout the USA in 1866. The Civil War was a tragic chapter in America's short history that left 600,000 dead. Lincoln never got to savor victory—he was assassinated before the war's final shots were fired.

The Industrial Age

The wounded South struggled with reconstruction, a devastated economy, and a new social order. While slavery was formally abolished, emancipated slaves and their descendants continued to face hardship, segregation, and discrimination.

Fortunes were very different in the North. Here the Industrial Revolution transformed the USA into a major economic power. A new breed of business magnate, including J. P. Morgan, John D. Rockefeller, and Andrew Carnegie, built vast empires in banking, oil, and steel. America's new elite, they amassed great wealth and built opulent mansions. Claiming they were merely the "stewards of God's wealth" (and also mindful of antitrust legislation), they established America's generous tradition of philanthropy.

The late nineteenth century also brought a significant change in the demographic makeup. Adding to the stream of English, Irish, German, and Dutch settlers, immigrants from Central Europe flocked to work in the Northeast's factories, and the Chinese descended on California's gold mines.

Revolutionary advances in transportation and communication technology helped integrate the country, at the same time opening it up to new possibilities. The transcontinental railroad (1869), for example, carried western beef and wheat to the east, and settlers and manufactured goods back west.

As the developing country sprawled out, American cities began to rise up, and Louis Sullivan's steel-framed "skyscrapers" carved out Manhattan's legendary skyline.

An End to Isolationism

Having populated its interior and established itself as an economic power, America decided to expand its influence overseas. Alaska had been purchased from Russia in 1867. Victory in the Spanish-American War (1898) allowed the USA to expand its influence into the Caribbean and Pacific with the acquisition of Guam, the Philippines, and Puerto Rico, and control over Cuba. It further expanded its empire by annexing the sugar-producing islands of Hawaii (1898), and opening up the Panama Canal (1914).

It has been noted that, when it came to US commercial expansionism, the dollar has never been "isolationist." But when it came to the military and political affairs of other countries, America had long pursued the isolationist stance outlined by President Monroe in 1823. This ended in 1917, three years into the First World War, when the German decision to attack neutral shipping prompted President Wilson to enter the conflict. The massive injection of American troops to bolster the depleted Allied ranks was decisive in securing peace in November 1918.

The Great Depression

The 1920s were boom years for the economy, with America acquiring the taste for mass consumption of mass-produced goods. When Henry Ford first introduced his Model T car to the country, it was love at first sight. With the advent of Hollywood motion pictures, images of the "American Dream" were exported around the world.

But the unchecked growth of the economy led to rampant speculation. On October 24, 1929, the stock market collapsed, plunging the nation into the Great Depression. Many lost their businesses and life savings. Farmers weren't spared, as a drought destroyed crops and livelihoods. The New Deal policies of Franklin Delano Roosevelt provided relief, but recovery was agonizingly slow.

AN END TO DYNASTIC SUCCESSION?

"FDR"—President Franklin Roosevelt—was related to his predecessor "Teddy" Roosevelt, but only distantly. They were fifth cousins. Oddly, FDR's wife, Eleanor, was a closer relative. She was Teddy's niece and was already named Roosevelt before she married Franklin.

Other related presidents include the Adamses (father and son), the Harrisons (grandfather and grandson) and the Bushes (father and son). Former First Lady Hillary Rodham Clinton might have clinched the first husband and wife pairing, but she lost to Donald Trump in the Electoral College, despite winning the popular vote in the 2016 election.

"Into the Jaws of Death": US infantrymen raid Nazi-held beaches at Omaha, France, June 1944.

The Second World War

American isolationism was tested once again when Britain declared war on the German Nazi regime in September 1939. Recalcitrance ended with the Japanese attack on Pearl Harbor, Hawaii, on December 7, 1941, propelling America overnight into the Second World War. The war in Europe ended in May, 1945, but raged on in the Pacific until August, when the US dropped atomic bombs on Japan, at Hiroshima and Nagasaki. America justified the action by saying the alternative, an invasion of Japan, would have incurred greater losses on both sides.

The Cold War

If anyone was in any doubt, the establishment of the Marshall Plan (1947) and the creation of NATO (1949), committing American capital and troops to the reconstruction and defense of a democratic Europe, signaled a clear end to US isolationism.

The rapid spread of totalitarian regimes in postwar Eastern Europe and the Communist takeover in China alarmed Americans. Playing up the paranoia to justify his "Communist containment" foreign policy, President Truman ordered Senator Joseph McCarthy to investigate and expose all "Communist subversives" living on American soil.

Concerns over expanding Communist influence in Asia led to US military intervention in Korea (1950–53) and later Vietnam (1964–75). The competition between the Soviets and Americans for the mantle of "superpower" also resulted in a dangerous proliferation of atomic and later nuclear weapons. In 1962, in one of the most serious confrontations, President Kennedy ordered the Soviets to remove nuclear missiles from Cuban bases. After a tense standoff, Russia's President Khrushchev backed down, and nuclear war was averted. A grateful nation was grief-stricken the following year when the popular young president was assassinated by a Soviet sympathizer.

The Turbulent Sixties

Riding the popular sentiment following JFK's 1963 assassination while visiting Dallas, Texas, new president Lyndon Johnson introduced a bold program of civil rights legislation, ending racial segregation. But America's growing involvement in the Vietnam War polarized the nation, which became increasingly convinced that stemming the Communist tide half a world away was no justification for the loss of 58,000 American lives. Under

Civil rights leader Martin Luther King speaks at a press conference, March 1964.

mounting pressure, President Nixon signed a peace treaty with North Vietnam in 1973. The returning troops met with an indifferent reception; it wasn't until 1982 that wounds had healed sufficiently to erect the Vietnam War Memorial in the nation's capital, honoring the fallen.

Back home, Dr. Martin Luther King Jr., leader and lightning rod for the continuing Civil Rights movement, was assassinated in 1968, the same year as another social activist, Senator Robert Kennedy.

The sixties "counterculture" also produced advances in the rights of women, gays and lesbians, and immigrant workers. The tumultuous decade ended with a rare moment of unity when, in 1969, the USA successfully landed a man on the Moon.

Watergate to Monicagate

His significant foreign policy achievements overshadowed by the Watergate scandal, Nixon resigned in 1974. Despite the success of President Jimmy Carter (1976–80) in securing the Camp David Egyptian–Israeli peace agreement, the energy crisis and the American hostage drama in Iran sank his administration. The two terms of the popular President Reagan (1980–88) were characterized by a conservative social agenda, interventionist foreign policy, and deficit-inducing tax cuts.

The early 1990s witnessed a return to military intervention overseas, as Iraq's invasion of Kuwait prompted President George Bush (1988–92) to unleash the technological warfare of Desert Storm. Though victorious abroad, Bush was defeated by Bill Clinton (1992–2000), who was able to capitalize on domestic challenges. Despite being dogged by scandal, leading to his unsuccessful impeachment, Clinton had solid public support throughout his two terms, buoyed primarily by a booming economy.

9/11 and Its Consequences

The USA entered the twenty-first century as the world's only superpower—but with a new, faceless foe. The devastating attacks of September 11, 2001 that destroyed the World Trade Center in New York and damaged the Pentagon in Washington, D.C., killed 2,800 people on American soil, prompting President George W. Bush (2000–2008)—son of the former President George Bush— to take military action in Afghanistan and Iraq. The War on Terror overseas and the response to "9/11" at home dominated most of the two-term Bush presidency. In 2005, the city of New Orleans was devastated when flood controls failed following a direct hit by Hurricane Katrina.

It was a historic moment in 2009 when Democrat Barack Obama (2009–2017) became the first African-

WHY "9/11"?

The day that saw the destruction of the World
Trade Center's twin towers in downtown
Manhattan and serious damage to the Pentagon
quickly picked up the name "9/11." To understand
why, you need to know two facts about America.

First, Americans write dates with the month
preceding the day: September 11, 2001, not 11th
September 2001. When this is abbreviated to all
numbers, it becomes 9/11/01. (In the UK this
would mean the ninth of November.)

Second, the telephone number for the
emergency services through the United States is
911, pronounced "nine-one-one." The all-number
date is pronounced "nine-eleven," but the peculiar
coincidence was enough for it to become the
common label for a day of horror and sadness that
no American can ever forget.

American president of the United States, inheriting the
largest recession since the 1920s and a political and
cultural climate that was increasingly polarized. He also
picked up a Nobel Peace Prize in his first year in office!
His first term saw his signature Affordable Care Act
("Obamacare") enacted and signed into law, which
afforded health insurance to some 20 million people.
His second term saw the legalization of same-sex marriage
and the 2015 Paris Agreement to fight climate change.

He also normalized US relations with Cuba after fifty-four years of hostility. In 2011, Osama Bin Laden, founder of the extreme Islamist Al-Qaeda movement that carried out the 9/11 attacks, was assassinated by US Navy SEALs at his hideout in Pakistan.

The Trump Years

Donald Trump was a businessman and well-known media personality who, despite having neither political nor military experience, rose to the presidency in 2017. His fame, his ambition, and his brash, uncompromising style were welcomed by Republican voters and their representatives in Congress, who since the nineties had grown progressively less inclined to seek common ground with their Democratic colleagues.

During his presidential term, Trump introduced the biggest corporate tax cuts in history, lifted environmental regulations, and reshaped the federal judiciary. His dominant rallying cry, certainly in the many raucous rallies that continued after his inauguration, was his promise to build a wall along the USA's southern border to combat illegal immigration. He adopted the slogan "Make American Great Again"—abbreviated to MAGA, which you may still see on baseball caps. However, his public chiding of NATO members and admiration for autocratic leaders such as Russia's Vladimir Putin and North Korea's Kim Jong II led to tense relations with America's traditional allies. An impeachment in 2019 was defeated by the loyalty of Republicans in Congress.

Attacking the Capitol

In the November 2020 election, thanks to a massive turnout by his grass-roots conservative base, Trump received more than 74 million votes, beating Obama's 2008 record by nearly five million votes. But it still wasn't enough to beat Democrat Joe Biden's 81 million votes.

Trump's groundless refusal to accept the loss had unprecedented consequences. On January 6, 2021—two weeks before Biden's scheduled inauguration—at a midday rally near the White House, Trump continued to cite false claims of election irregularities. Many of his supporters marched to the US Capitol, half a mile along Pennsylvania Avenue, where a joint session of Congress was counting the final electoral votes. About 2,500 of these supporters stormed the building, resulting in looting, vandalism, and tragically, five deaths. Some of the intruders carried signs for "QAnon," a conspiratorial political movement that had spread surreal claims accepted by many Trump devotees with a far-right outlook. Order was restored and Joe Biden's victory was confirmed by the re-assembled Congress at 3:24 a.m. the next morning.

Hundreds of attackers faced criminal charges in the following months, and in the last days of his presidency, Trump received a second impeachment. He was acquitted again, largely on party lines. He also snubbed his successor's inauguration, the first president in more than 150 years to do so.

Biden Takes Over

At age 78, Joe Biden—after thirty-six years a senator and

President Joe Biden takes the oath of office at his inauguration ceremony, January 2021.

eight years as Obama's VP—was the oldest president in history to take the helm. His own VP, Kamala Harris, is the first woman, the first Asian American, and the first African American to assume the role. (Her mother is from India, her father from Jamaica.)

Biden immediately reversed Trump's decision to extricate America from the Paris Climate Agreement and the World Health Organization, introduced a major stimulus package for American jobs and infrastructure, stopped all work on the border wall, and finally withdrew the last American troops from Afghanistan. But his early presidency was dominated by the crushing impact of the coronavirus pandemic on life and work in the USA and by Russia's brutal invasion of neighboring Ukraine.

COVID-19 IN AMERICA

The first officially recorded Covid-19 case in the USA appeared only three weeks after the virus was initially detected in Wuhan, China, in December 2019. By the end of January 2020, President Trump had declared a public health emergency, and travel restrictions to and from China were imposed.

By February 2020 the virus had claimed its first US fatalities. Despite Trump's optimistic forecast of an imminent end to the pandemic throughout the early months of the year, by March it was clear the virus was spreading fast and its status was lifted to that of a "national emergency."

Americans were advised not to travel abroad and to restrict the size of gatherings, while states and local authorities imposed mask mandates and stay-at-home "lockdowns," which included school closures. The infection rate and subsequent death toll continued to rise— Covid-19's mortality rate was declared to be ten times higher than the common flu, reaching 100,000 deaths by the end of May. Intensive Care Units in hospitals became overwhelmed by cases. Tightly packed Manhattan was an early hotspot, so much so that authorities erected a field hospital in Central Park for the potential overflow of infected patients. Testing centers sprung up across the nation.

The nationwide quarantine caused an inevitable economic contraction. Unemployment levels reached record highs as struggling companies were forced to lay off workers, and the freshly homebound became acquainted with what was to become the newest national pastime: Zoom meetings.

The first vaccines for the virus were approved by the Food and Drug Administration in August that same year, and a national vaccination program began in December. By then, one out of every twenty-two Americans had tested positive for the virus. One month later it was one in thirteen.

Incoming President Joe Biden immediately pumped $1.9 trillion into a range of recovery initiatives, and in his first television address following his inauguration in January 2021, he challenged states to administer one shot of the vaccine to all adults by May 1. Booster shots were subsequently introduced. Meanwhile, the infection rate continued to ebb and flow with the arrival of new virus variations—Alpha in December 2020, Delta in April 2021, Omicron and its subvariants in November 2021—leading to shifting guidance from states and cities on mask-wearing and quarantine.

Interesting to note is that despite the wide availability of free vaccines, by April 2022, nearly a quarter of all Americans still hadn't had one. Why? Well, that's most likely explained by the highly independent and sometimes anti-authoritarian streak in the American character that resists being told what to do (more on that in Chapter 2). It's largely for this reason that, though the virus death rate had dropped significantly, it hadn't done so as quickly as in other developed countries.

Make sure to check the current procedures before you travel to the United States. This will most likely include proof that you're vaccinated and that you don't currently have the virus. You may find that a new variation temporarily delays your visit, depending on your status and location.

CHAPTER TWO

VALUES &
ATTITUDES

What really matters to Americans? It might seem impossible to generalize across vast distances and a population of the more than 330 million who are renowned for being highly individualistic. Yet the special character and unique experiences of the early settlers and successive waves of immigrants have indeed shaped a set of all-American values.

AMERICA—THE IDEAL

In his book *American Exceptionalism*, Seymour Lipset observes that America is the only nation in the world that is founded on a creed. Unlike societies where nationality is related to accident of birth, becoming an American is more of a conscious act, an ideological commitment to a set of values and a way of life.

Despite their different backgrounds or motivations, the founders who came willingly to America were bound together by similar beliefs, united in the same mission.

They rejected notions of a state-mandated religion, a powerful centralized government, or a rigid class structure. Their utopian ideal was to have the space and freedom to live their lives according to their religion, without government interference. They believed that morality and hard work led to the improvement of mankind and the betterment of society. Everyone had an equal chance of success because every individual was free to control his own destiny. (Well, at that time, every white male, anyway.)

These guiding principles of liberty, equality—even the "pursuit of happiness"—were modeled and reinforced by many of colonial America's early leaders. Later institutionalized in the Declaration of Independence and the Constitution, they continue to shape public policy and national values.

EQUALITY OF OPPORTUNITY

Early on, Americans were determined to make their new society a meritocracy. First enshrined in the Declaration of Independence, the phrase "all men are created equal" emphasized that, regardless of religion or background, every individual should be provided with equal opportunity to succeed. Rungs on the ladder of success would not be arbitrarily allocated by birthright, but achieved through initiative and perseverance. It took some time—and considerable struggle—for the rhetoric to become reality, but America is now a nation that has formally ended all barriers based on gender, race, religion, and national origin, and it's progressing on sexual orientation.

Equal opportunity isn't to be confused with egalitarianism (another important American value that we'll discuss). In his book *Democracy in America* (1835) de Tocqueville first observed that emphasis is placed on equality of opportunity—not equal conditions for all. Consistent with their individualistic mentality, Americans believe that ability, effort, and achievement should be rewarded, and they're wary of the notion of government interference to iron out social and economic inequities. Rather than investing in a European-style welfare state, America aims to "level the playing field" and promotes upward mobility by making its educational system flexible and accessible to all, at least in the early stages.

INDIVIDUALISM

The right to control your own destiny is a cherished American value. Individual rights and freedoms are fiercely defended. While the conformist Japanese warn that "the nail that sticks up gets hammered down," Americans believe that "the squeaky wheel gets the grease." In other words, speak up, get yourself noticed, and you'll get your needs met.

How can a nation of individualists also be team players? The American notion of "group" or "team" affiliation is different from that of collectivist countries. While fully committed to the team's goal, individuals will also use group membership to advance a personal agenda—to showcase their talents. From the conference room to the locker room, individual members will still expect to be rewarded based on individual contribution, with the star player receiving the lion's share. It's fun to be a part of a team and great things can be achieved together, but at the end of the day you have to "look out for number one," and once the group no longer serves the individual's purpose, it's time to move on, "no strings attached."

Americans like their social and collective activities to be voluntary and local. The proud and generous supporter of a church outreach program or community charity will also be a vociferous opponent of government programs that use tax income to bolster welfare. Relief spending to assist low-income families during the coronavirus pandemic was viewed as a necessary exception by many conservatives, who otherwise believe the government spends too much on the poor.

SELF-RELIANCE

Stemming from individualism and the hardships and isolation endured by those early settlers, Americans value self-reliance and a "can-do" spirit. After all, the nation is largely descended from triple-tested pioneer stock: their forebears found the courage to uproot themselves from their ancestral homes in Europe, survived a perilous sea voyage, and then may have forged their way across an unfamiliar and "untamed" continent in search of a new life. Resilience is in the American genes.

The notion that "God helps those who help themselves" greatly inspired the American work ethic in its early years. This has evolved into a mentality of "self-help" in seeking solutions to modern-day challenges. Good American parents instill this value by offering their children every opportunity to prepare for adulthood, then launching them out of the nest to make their own way in the world. In most communities, elderly people prefer to remain self-reliant, too. They would rather live in a retirement community or nursing home than become dependent on family members. In the same vein, practical assistance is given to the physically or mentally disabled to allow them to lead independent lives and develop their full potential.

THAT "CAN DO" SPIRIT

"The Yankee means to make moonlight work, if he can."
Ralph Waldo Emerson, 1846

The adventurous and industrious types who conquered America believed that constant change was not an option but a duty, and that progress was its reward. This mindset has shaped a future-oriented culture that rewards "go-getters" who "think out of the box" and "push the envelope." With vision, energy, and perseverance, anything can be accomplished. It's a conviction that's placed a man on the Moon and produced three times as many Nobel prize winners as the next country. It's why the introduction of a new device or brand of washing powder is automatically and enthusiastically embraced. If it's new, it must be improved.

Fatalistic cultures believe that bad luck is inevitable and destiny is determined by the fickle finger of fate. To Americans, that's superstitious claptrap. Rather than passively reacting to events, Americans prefer to take control by being proactive. They have perfected the art of predicting, diagnosing, and controlling every aspect of life.

To be in control, it helps to have nature on your side. Some cultures live in harmony with their environment. Americans like to wrestle it to the ground and harness its power for their own personal use. Wind, sun, and ocean waves are transformed into valuable energy sources; state-of-the-art heating and air-conditioning systems allow Alaskans and Floridians to enjoy the same room temperatures all year round.

That obsession with control extends to time. Time is money, and so it should be spent wisely, not frittered away. Lawyers bill by the minute, and local TV news channels boast they can cover international news in one minute flat. "Beating the clock" is less about punctuality and more about the efficient use of time. Smartphones offer dozens of calendar apps and let you fire off a text or a tweet whenever a thought strikes you. With Internet hotspots ubiquitous from coast to coast, "downtime" has to be a choice, not an excuse. As the saying goes, "If you want something done, give it to a busy person."

Unwavering optimism and faith in the future inspire not only action but a confident swagger and upbeat tone— today is good, but tomorrow can only be better.

VOX POPULI

In colonial America, populism took root as local citizens met in town halls to discuss community issues. Antagonism toward a distant colonial authority that imposed rule from the top-down inspired Americans to create a system that would work from the grass roots up—a government "of the people, by the people," to use Abraham Lincoln's words.

Today, more public offices are elected positions, and elections and referendums are held more often than in any other country—the *Economist* estimated about one million in each four-year election cycle. Citizens make their voices heard in council chambers and town meetings, populate local school boards, take up causes, and sow "grass-roots" political activity.

EGALITARIANISM

Consistent with the belief that "all men are born equal," American social relations are founded on equal respect and informality. In an early example of egalitarianism, the Congress of 1789 decided that George Washington should be addressed simply as "Mr. President." Today's corporate CEO is referred to as Elon or Kathy, and telemarketers expect to be on first-name terms with you, too.

Is America a classless society? Yes and no. While social stratification does exist, the concept of class is entirely different in America. In the traditional societies of Europe, class denotes an inherited station in life. Here, it's an acquired status—a position earned through effort and achievement. As such, social standing isn't defined by accent, affiliations, or geography, but by money and power. To Americans, these are symbols of status and success. There's also far less deference to authority, and fewer privileges based on rank.

While the number of Americans who identify as "middle class" has shrunk in recent years, financial success has augmented a self-identified upper class. Largely a political label, "middle class" is most often used to describe any hard-working supporter of American values who wants to see his or her family advance, from doctors and lawyers to builders and baristas, many of whom would be considered "working class" in other countries.

WORK ETHIC

> *"Work: 1. That which keeps us out of trouble.*
> *2. A plan of God to circumvent the Devil"*
> The Roycroft Dictionary &
> Book of Epigrams, 1923

The Protestant work ethic provided a clear and compelling equation for the early settlers: hard work led to a moral life, spiritual fulfillment, and God's blessing in the form of material rewards here on earth. Benjamin Franklin (a Founding Father who never became president) encapsulated much of the work ethic in *Poor Richard's Almanack* (1736), coining sayings still used today, such as "Early to bed, early to rise, makes a man healthy, wealthy, and wise," and "Time is money." Today, the average American still works three hundred hours a year more than the average European, with shorter lunch breaks and much less vacation time.

Unlike "work to live" cultures, where work is just one of the many dimensions of one's life, for many Americans work is central in defining their sense of identity and self-worth. Even those who can afford to step off the treadmill often don't.

In this land of abundance, success didn't have to be gained at the expense of others—excepting always the experience of the Native Americans and Black people who were forced to work as slaves. Of course, many have a "leg up" by being born into privilege, but, in theory at least, anyone can make a million or go to Harvard in this socially mobile society. Indeed, America reveres those who have risen from humble beginnings and overcome adversity to achieve success. There's also rarely any guilt attached to enjoying the "fruits of one's labors," which is why Americans can envy the extremely wealthy without necessarily resenting them. There is, however, a growing sentiment that there's something troubling in the ever-widening disparity in the incomes of the mega rich and the Average Joe.

CONSERVATISM AND MORALITY

More than a third of Americans describe themselves as "conservative," and they more or less form the dependable base of the Republican Party, committed to low taxes and limited government interference and spending—apart from whatever it costs to sustain a strong military. For the American right, Ronald Reagan's presidency was both the pinnacle and a golden era of modern politics, though for a narrower slice of the "further right," that was eclipsed by Donald Trump.

But conservatism is more than a political viewpoint. In America, it has its own unique meaning that embraces the social, cultural, and religious lives of its believers. Those founding values of self-reliance and individualism combine with an unshakable respect for tradition and the law. This may be strengthened further by the Bible-centered moral teachings of the Protestant Evangelical churches, with their Puritan values and suspicion of secularism and, indeed, any science that challenges God's hands-on role in history.

Americans tend to view morality in absolute terms. Whereas in Europe, abortion and gay rights are regarded as political issues, in the USA they're defined in moral and ethical terms, increasingly polarizing the nation and provoking emotional debate.

The "red states," where conservatism reigns, cluster in the center of the country, and visitors whose only experience of Americans comes from major cities of New York and California—noted liberal hotbeds—shouldn't assume they've witnessed the full range of the social and political spectrum.

What does all this mean for the foreign visitor? A lot of variation on "moral" issues from state to state, and an ever-evolving national consensus on these issues that may seem surprisingly behind the times to, say, Europeans who tend to be much more tolerant of gun control and convinced about global warming.

GIVING BACK

When John F. Kennedy, in his 1960 inaugural address, exhorted Americans, "Ask not what your country can do for you, ask what you can do for your country," he was preaching to the choir. The USA outstrips every other

Activists take part in a food giveaway for families in Georgia, December 2020.

nation in terms of time and money donated to worthy causes. One in four American adults volunteer their time on a regular basis. The combination of America's generosity and "can do" attitude produced charitable contributions from individuals and corporations of $471 billion in 2020 alone, despite the financial difficulties many faced that year as a result of the coronavirus pandemic. ("Charitable" contributions are the generally tax-free donations to "not-for-profit" organizations, which may be cultural, educational, religious, or for medical research, as well as those that provide charity to the needy.)

The first volunteer organizations were faith-based groups that assumed responsibility for the social welfare programs usually administered by the government in other nations. Today individuals from all walks of life donate privately or organize charity events through their work, school, or community group. Every weekend thousands run to fight global hunger, or walk to buy a new roof for the local church. Even more telling, busy Americans donate time to help those in need. Many young people volunteer to serve in the Peace Corps, founded by President Kennedy, which currently provides assistance in more than sixty countries, while AmeriCorps gives similar opportunities for service within the USA.

What motivates this constant outpouring of generosity? Americans get to apply their skills and energy, "give back" to the community, and make a difference. In return, conscience, body, and wallet all get a good workout, and society is self-supporting—not reliant on government handouts. It's a win-win proposition for all.

DIVERSITY

Americans proudly assert that "in diversity there is strength." There's also challenge. Legislation and increased social awareness have led to greater equality, regardless of race, ethnicity, creed, gender, sexual orientation, or disability—on paper, at least. But in an immigrant nation that is fiercely proud of its many ancestral cultures, progress on integration can be slow. Change in societal attitudes can be measured in the use of more respectful terminology for minorities, the spread of multilingual signs and services, and corporate initiatives both to promote diversity in the workplace and to respond swiftly to bigotry.

Affirmative action initiatives, ensuring that employers and educational institutions allocate a designated number of places to minority groups, have attempted to redress injustices in the system. Some people, however, counter that this constitutes "reverse discrimination" and advocate race-neutral alternatives. The ideal of equality of opportunity continues to bump up against the reality of existing socio-economic inequities and lingering discrimination. For example, Black drivers are still 20 percent more likely to be pulled over by cops than their white counterparts and nearly twice as likely to be searched. Movements like Black Lives Matter exist to protest injustices when they occur, such as in the case of African-American George Floyd. His murder by Minneapolis police in 2020 brought the issue of racial discrimination to the fore and instigated a wider societal self-reckoning that continues today.

Veterans salute at a Memorial Day ceremony.

PATRIOTISM

Post-Revolutionary Americans had neither a long-shared history nor a common cause to rally around once they had expelled the British. A sense of identity and unity had to be forged. The Constitution and the flag soon became patriotism's most potent symbols.

To the visitor, the American flag seems to be everywhere. It not only flies outside public buildings but graces many a front lawn. The national anthem is a story about the flag that flew throughout the night during the British bombardment of Baltimore's Fort McHenry in 1812, which you can still see at the Museum of American History in Washington, D.C; it represents the strength of the American spirit. Schoolchildren pledge allegiance to the flag, and when the national anthem plays, people stand, and many place their hands on their hearts.

As guests in America, how should visitors react to the American predilection for wearing their patriotism on their sleeve? By going with the flow, leaving the jaded cynicism at home, occasionally biting their tongue, and demonstrating a sympathetic understanding of the historical and cultural forces that have shaped the deep sense of national pride. At the same time, visitors shouldn't be offended if an American seems to know little of (to them) foreign customs or habits. They'll make up for any apparent ignorance of life outside the USA with politeness and a willingness to learn.

These Colors Don't Run

The Stars and Stripes is more than a flag. Other nations may have a figurehead monarch or a clutch of ancient traditions, but for Americans, "Old Glory" is by far the most potent symbol of a nation that takes its patriotism seriously. Don't be surprised to see it fluttering on poles outside many private homes.

As you've read, the flag is the core of the national anthem and the focus of every schoolchild's daily pledge. Its stripes represent the thirteen original colonies, its stars number the current states (prompting twenty-six redesigns since the flag's initial design in 1777). There are strict rules governing the way it is displayed, folded, and even disposed of.

CHAPTER THREE

CUSTOMS & TRADITIONS

SEPARATION OF CHURCH AND STATE

At American award ceremonies, tearful Country and Western singers, hip-hop stars, and Oscar winners often thank God in their acceptance speeches. The depth and pervasiveness of spiritual life in America is surprising to many outsiders. Like many aspects of US culture, religion is full of contradictions and paradoxes, New World adaptations of Old World influences, and amazing diversity.

One of the first acts of the fledgling American government was to decree the separation of Church and State: "Congress shall make no law respecting an establishment of religion, or prohibiting the free exercise thereof." In theory, this First Amendment to the Constitution ensured that there'd be no official government-backed religion. Individuals were free to observe whatever faith they chose.

In practice, Supreme Court justices constantly struggle to determine what constitutes government meddling in religious matters (and vice versa). One glaring contradiction is that while prayer is not allowed in public schools, students recite the "pledge of allegiance" on a daily basis, which contains the line "one nation under God" (although those last two words were only added in 1954 as an anti-communist gesture). Similarly, even though the government isn't supposed to endorse any one religion, new sessions of Congress begin with a prayer, the president ends speeches with "God bless America," and the national motto, adopted in 1956, is "In God We Trust." The controversy has been characterized as pitting civic duty against individual conscience—one cherished American value against another.

Religious Affiliations

Seventy-two percent of Americans express some religious affiliation, although only 20 percent say their faith is the most important thing in their lives and only 28 percent claim to attend services regularly. Religion has always been a voluntary activity in the USA, so those who practice their faith do so by choice, as a matter of individual conscience. This may account for the depth of fundamentalism and the wide variety of religions. With nearly two hundred active religious sects, religion in the United States is a buyer's market, and about half of American adults will change their religious affiliation during their lives, 28 percent leaving the faith in which they were raised for another or discarding it completely.

In 2020, Protestant denominations constituted 46.6 percent of the population. It's worth noting, however, that Protestantism covers a vast spectrum, with the formal Episcopalian and severe Lutheran doctrines at one extreme and the exuberant gospel-singing Southern Baptist Churches at the other. Many "evangelical" Christians have embraced Prosperity Theology, dating back to the 1950s, which teaches that God wants us to be wealthy, a belief that dovetails well with American conservative values. Megachurches attract worshipers in their thousands. Other ministries use mass media to spread the word and seek donations through "televangelism," which is still going strong despite the occasional juicy scandal. For many televangelists, the line between religion and politics is often blurred.

Catholics remains the single largest denomination with 20.8 percent. Many Catholic families send their children to parochial (Catholic) schools, which offer strict academic and disciplinary standards and the freedom to hold religious services.

Most of the country's 7.6 million Jews (approximately 2 percent of the population) belong to one of three denominations—Orthodox, Conservative, or Reform, with the Orthodox being most observant in terms of diet, lifestyle, and religious practice, and Reform the most liberal. Many Jewish children attend school in the public (government) system but receive religious instruction at a Hebrew school. There are also many nonreligious Jews who still derive a strong sense of identity and community from their Jewish ethnicity.

American adherents to Islam number approximately 3.85 million and make up some 1.2 percent of the population. The 9/11 attacks in 2001 increased the nation's fear of homegrown extremism, and this saw discrimination increase as a result, a pattern that repeated during Trump's presidency. However, American Muslims are well integrated in society, and their participation in public and political life has increased in recent years.

Buddhism and Hinduism are next in order of size, each with approximately one percent of the population.

The climate of tolerance and renewal in America fostered the growth of new religious movements among the early settlers. Surviving examples are the Church of Jesus Christ of Latter Day Saints (Mormons), Seventh Day Adventists, and Jehovah's Witnesses. Although many religious Americans question whether these qualify as truly "Christian" denominations, Republican candidate Mitt Romney's Mormonism hardly surfaced as an issue during his ill-fated 2012 presidential run.

One generalization that perhaps can be applied is that Americans of all faiths have regarded the Church as having a major responsibility in building communities, tackling social challenges, and helping the disenfranchised. Many of the hungry are fed, the homeless sheltered, and children and elderly people cared for by volunteers from religious institutions.

Some strictly religious sects have remained cohesive, homogeneous communities identifiable by their distinctive garb, such as the Amish and Mennonites in Pennsylvania and the Hassidim in New York. By and large, however, it's difficult to ascertain either religious affiliation or degree of observance based on appearance and lifestyle. A word of caution: Americans can be uncomfortable discussing their faith, so it should be considered off-limits in conversation with a new acquaintance.

New Hybrid Religions

Multicultural America has always been adept at adapting and combining the cultural traditions imported by its immigrants. This has created fascinating fusions in cuisine, music, and even spirituality. The American quest for spiritual fulfillment is regarded by many as inseparable from other American ideals of control over destiny, self-actualization, and the capacity for reinvention.

Many Americans are no longer monotheistic, instead drawing on traditional belief systems, Eastern philosophies, and New Age practices to create a "pick 'n' mix" approach to fulfilling spiritual and lifestyle needs. Forms of medicine, exercise, and diet previously thought of as "alternative" are now considered mainstream.

HATCHED, MATCHED, AND DISPATCHED

The rituals surrounding births, marriages, and deaths will again be influenced by the religious affiliation, if any, of the participants. Interfaith marriage is commonplace, and it's not unusual to have a priest and a rabbi co-officiating, or a licensed "marriage celebrant" conducting a secular service. The style of wedding is often a matter of personal taste and budget. In America weddings can take place anywhere, even in the back yard. The celebration can range from a New-Age barefoot ceremony on a California beach to a ritualized Greek Orthodox service in Chicago, or a designer-clad sophisticated affair at a New York hotel. In most places, the officiant is a licensed clergyman or justice of the peace, but some states license other people.

Weddings are often highly choreographed, with grand entrances into the church or reception space—often set to dance music—for the bridesmaids and groomsmen. Even the future in-laws get their moments in the spotlight.

One common American custom is for family, friends, and colleagues to throw a surprise baby or wedding "shower" for an expectant mother or bride-to-be. This involves baby- or wedding-related decorations, games and a cake, and the "showering" of gifts upon the guest of honor. And later, parents-to-be may throw their own "gender-reveal" party, with either pink (for a girl) or blue (for a boy) appearing when a cake is sliced into, a smoke bomb is detonated, or something even more spectacular.

Some other important rites of passage observed in American life are religious, such as the Christian First Communion and Jewish Bar Mitzvah (for boys) and Bat Mitzvah (for girls). Others, such as the Hispanic Quinceaneros, or fifteenth-birthday girls' parties, are ethnically based, but elaborate "sweet sixteen" birthday celebrations for girls occur in all cultures. Perhaps the most commonly shared, and fondly remembered, milestone in a young person's life is Prom Night— celebrating high-school graduation at eighteen.

Rising to the Occasion

Not just weddings! Americans "ceremonialize" everything, upping the significance of every occasion by doing it big. Annual milestones such as Valentine's Day and Halloween always get the full treatment. Nursery schools have graduation ceremonies. Kids fill display cases in their homes with trophies, sometimes awarded just for showing up at a sporting event. Even the two-second coin toss to decide who gets to kick off at the Superbowl has its own mini-show, with TV graphics, a line-up of guest observers, and a specially minted coin.

HOLIDAYS—WHAT THEY ARE AND HOW THEY ARE CELEBRATED

While most American holidays are observed nationwide, they are in fact mandated by individual states, and the way in which they're celebrated is influenced by religious affiliation, ethnic background, and regional culture. In practice, most states observe the eleven federal public holidays, when schools, commercial and retail banks, post offices, and government offices will be closed. (On certain holidays, the stock markets may stay open.) Transportation and other services may operate on a reduced schedule. Private companies don't always recognize federal holidays and may offer staff alternative days off, such as the Friday after Thanksgiving.

KEY HOLIDAYS AND CELEBRATIONS

New Year's Day*	January 1
Martin Luther King Jr. Day*	third Monday in January
Valentine's Day	February 14
President's Day*	third Monday in February
St. Patrick's Day	March 17
Good Friday and Easter Monday	dates vary
Memorial Day*	fourth Monday in May
Juneteenth*	June 19
Independence Day*	July 4
Labor Day*	first Monday in September
Columbus Day/ Indigenous Peoples' Day*	second Monday in October
Halloween	October 31
Veteran's Day*	November 11
Thanksgiving*	fourth Thursday in November
Christmas Day*	December 25

*These days are generally public holidays. If any holiday with a fixed date falls on a weekend, the preceding Friday or following Monday is usually given as a holiday from work.

Some holidays are uniquely American, such as Thanksgiving and Independence Day. But although they're not official holidays, many religious or ethnic festivals imported by immigrants have also assumed a distinctively American identity. A case in point is St. Patrick's Day, when Americans of all ethnicities don

Pipe bands take part in the annual St. Patrick's Day parades held across America.

something green, possibly eat or drink something green that isn't usually green, and claim to be of Irish descent!

A cynic might say that many of these celebrations, particularly the religious ones, have lost their original meaning and are kept alive by family tradition and Hallmark marketing. Certainly, it seems that no sooner has the St. Patrick's Day green beer gone flat than the plastic "Kiss me I'm Irish" hats are replaced by Easter eggs in store windows.

Cynicism aside, no one mounts a parade, loves the razzmatazz, or gets into the spirit of holidays more than Americans. A holiday is an opportunity to exhibit their patriotism, a coming together to reaffirm their identity and unity. On Memorial Day, Veteran's Day, and Presidents' Day, for example, "Old Glory," the American flag, will be much in evidence. Holidays also mark the rhythm of the seasons. Memorial Day and Labor Day "bookend" the summer season (the latter holiday weekend often devoted to frantic back-to-school shopping).

In addition to national holidays, there are countless other events ranging from small-town celebrations to countywide affairs. Street parades, often headed by majorettes leading a marching band, demonstrate a uniquely American combination of individualism, competition, and team cooperation.

Communities hold festivals to celebrate whatever it is that has put them on the map. Practically every food, dance, and ethnic group is celebrated with a festival. Polka festivals are held in the North, catfish festivals in the South, and German Oktoberfests in practically every state!

Martin Luther King Jr. Day and Juneteenth

The two most recent additions to the list of federal holidays celebrate Black history. The Reverend Martin Luther King Jr (1929–1968) is honored on the third Monday in January, close to (and occasionally on) his January 15 birthday. King's message of nonviolent resistance and his tragic assassination led to major advances in civil rights for minorities. His holiday—often abbreviated to MLK Day— was first celebrated in 1986. Juneteenth meanwhile had been commemorated in the African-American community for more than one hundred and fifty years before becoming a federal holiday in 2021. The date, June 19, marks the day in 1865 that African Americans living in Confederate states finally received the news that slavery had been abolished.

Valentine's Day—February 14

Historians disagree on who exactly St. Valentine was, but commercial Valentine cards were first sent in the early 1800s by Miss Esther Howland—an American! February 14 has become a day for Americans to give cards, flowers, and candy to the ones they love. It isn't a national holiday, but it surpasses even Christmas for the amount of mail it generates. Couples will plan a romantic dinner, and it's the most popular date on which to propose marriage. Cards and gifts are also exchanged between classmates, and parents and their children.

Fourth of July

This quintessentially American holiday commemorates the adoption of the US Declaration of Independence on July 4, 1776. America dresses up in the stars and stripes to celebrate its birthday. Everything from T-shirts to tablecloths is in red, white, and blue. Family and friends gather to enjoy barbecues and picnics against a backdrop of outdoor concerts and fireworks. Hot dogs, hamburgers, corn, and apple pie are the patriotic foods of choice.

A flag-adorned vintage car takes part in the Rose, White, and Blue July 4th Parade in San Jose, California.

Halloween—October 31

On Hallowmas (the feast of All Hallows' Eve—originally the pagan festival of Samhain, or "summer's end") people left out sweets to appease the souls of the dead, who were rumored to roam the earth the night before All Saints' Day. In its modern-day American incarnation, Halloween isn't a national holiday but has become a highly commercialized event. Wholesome suburban homes are transformed into haunted houses complete with spider webs, skeletons, and plastic tombstones. Children dress up in costumes, teenagers opting for the gruesome and gory while younger ones tend to favor cartoon characters and superheroes. They go from house to house "trick or treating"— demanding candy in return for not playing a prank on the homeowner. (Fail to provide the goodies and risk finding your house "egged" during the night or your trees and bushes "TP-ed"—festooned with toilet paper!)

If you're in New York City, don't miss the fun and inventive Halloween Parade in Greenwich Village, inspired by the Big Apple's LGBTQ community, where "anything goes."

Thanksgiving—Fourth Thursday in November

Thanksgiving is a uniquely North American holiday, initiated by the early settlers to give thanks for the abundant harvest that allowed them to survive. In the busiest travel period of the year, families reunite and enjoy a feast of traditional, indigenous foods, featuring turkey and dressing, cranberry sauce, candied yams, and pumpkin pie. New Thanksgiving traditions have evolved since the days of the Pilgrims, and the meal is usually sandwiched in

Macy's Thanksgiving Day Parade, New York.

between the national television broadcasts of the Macy's (New York) Thanksgiving Day parade in the morning, and a college football game in the afternoon.

Because American Thanksgiving is always a Thursday and families can end up far from home, the Friday that follows is usually taken as a vacation day. And what better way to spend it than making a start on Christmas? "Black Friday," the busiest shopping day of the year, is marked by sales and giveaways, and is now followed by "Cyber Monday." Finished your Thanksgiving turkey? Then take your campstool down to the mall, so you can be first in line for that new iPhone when stores open at four in the morning!

Christmas Day—December 25

Christians celebrate the birth of Jesus Christ on December 25, and for some people this may be the only time in the year when they attend church. Even the nonreligious celebrate, decorating their houses, putting up a Christmas tree, and gathering with family to exchange gifts and enjoy a special dinner. Unlike Thanksgiving, when there are few adaptations of traditional fare, the Christmas feast is heavily influenced by ethnic origins. Visit four neighboring households and you'll discover that German *pfeffernuesse*, Italian *crostoli*, Southern bread pudding, and American sugar cookies are all considered traditional Christmas dessert.

Happy Holidays to All

Those from predominantly Protestant or Catholic countries may be puzzled by the generic greeting "happy holidays" rather than something more specific, especially around Christmas. Since the country's inception, well before the advent of political correctness, Americans have respected the many other holidays observed by those of different religions, races, and ethnicities.

In December, for example, Jews celebrate Hanukkah, the eight-day Festival of Lights, and many African-Americans observe Kwanzaa (December 26 to January 1), a period of reflection and thanksgiving. Muslim communities will fast in the daylight hours during the holy month of Ramadan. For the Russian and Greek Orthodox Church, Easter is the most significant period in the religious year. Rosh Hashanah (the Jewish New Year) and Yom Kippur (the Day of Atonement) in September are the most sacred days of the year for Jews, while Passover in March or April is celebrated with the seder feast, an important family gathering.

Various nationalities or ethnic groups may also celebrate their own holidays. Mexico's Independence Day, Cinco de Mayo (May 5), is marked with parties and street parades in larger cities, including New York and Los Angeles. Chinese New Year in late January or early February is observed in the Chinatown districts of New York and San Francisco. The French quarter of New Orleans is the scene of decorated floats, elaborate costumes, and round-the-clock partying in celebration of Mardi Gras (or "Fat Tuesday," the beginning of Lent in late February or early March). Finally, the LGBTQ Pride parade is a colorful annual fixture in many cities, including New York and San Francisco, both in June.

CHAPTER FOUR

MAKING FRIENDS

Newcomers to this young country brought their distinct cultural traditions of hospitality, their own standards of politeness, their stakeout on the bashful-to-brash continuum. America never seems more diverse than when it makes a first impression, and the visitor may wonder if the carefree surfer dude on the beach in LA and the soft-spoken, thoughtful farmer in Minnesota are the same species, never mind the same nationality.

But that server in the New York deli who grunts at your "thank you" isn't being rude. He's just busy. And the woman who brought your breakfast in the Atlanta hotel isn't being insincere when her "have a nice day" wish gushes on for several sentences. She's just showing Southern politeness. Ask either of these people for assistance or information and they'll be glad to drop the attitude and help you.

So while this is an excellent time to remind you that with a subject as expansive and varied as the American people this book has to make many generalizations, you may find that when you go beyond that first impression, there really is such a thing as . . .

FRIENDSHIP, AMERICAN STYLE

Americans are among the most open, fun, friendly people on the planet, but their idea of what constitutes a friendship may be different from what you're used to.

Not for independent Americans is the sense of duty and mutual obligation that characterizes Asian relationships. They're far less likely to impose on a friend to seek help in getting a job or fixing their car. It seems people are always busy and frequently moving on, so friendships are often, by necessity, of a transitory nature. The attitude is to seize the day and enjoy the friendship while it lasts. If you run into a friend again after losing touch, time is spent happily catching up, not apologizing for the lack of contact. The best friendships are considered to be low maintenance and guilt free.

The warm smiles, the expressions of interest, the generous gestures are all genuine, and those used to Northern European reserve or the formal ritualized courtship of Asia may think making friends in the USA will be a breeze. Yet newcomers can be confused and disappointed to discover that a relationship may go no further than surface friendliness.

The good news is that this means you can feel free to accept—and extend—casual invitations. No plans for the weekend? You'll be readily invited to tag along to a ball game or party. You can relax and have fun without that nagging sense of indebtedness or need to reciprocate, which weighs on other cultures.

GETTING TO KNOW YOU

Americans like to hit the ground running when it comes to getting to know someone. Their seemingly personal questions may appear intrusive to some cultures. For example, "Where did you go to school?" might trigger the defenses of a class-bound Englishman. Here, it's simply an attempt to speed up the getting-to-know-you process. This works in your favor. Feel free to ask questions or engage in a conversation on safe topics, such as sports, family, hobbies, pets.

While many Americans are well traveled, they're in the minority: only about a third have an up-to-date passport. So don't be offended if a comment about your country or culture seems insulting—it's usually just a lack of information, and a gentle correction will be well taken. What if the conversation strays onto a topic you may find private, such as health or personal finances? Americans can't always take a subtle hint when they're being intrusive—a light-hearted comment and a change of subject will probably work. If you're from Europe, expect to hear how many ancestors from your country figure in your host's family tree. And if you're from Britain, that sudden odd way of speaking is probably an American's attempt to mimic your accent—it's meant to be playful, not mocking.

There's little in the United States that truly offends, other than criticizing the country's institutions or way of life, which probably isn't a good icebreaker in any country. American society has steadily grown more polarized in recent years, however, and Republican and Democrat voters are today less likely to respect the other side's outlook than they once were. As such, whether talking to friends or family, Americans increasingly prefer to dodge the topic of politics in conversation, and some confess to breaking off contact with friends who don't share their political views. Our advice? Steer clear. It might be wise to sidestep religion at first too, even if your host doesn't.

What will scare off an American? Perceived attempts to dominate their time or become overly dependent. It's important to read social cues, respect social boundaries, and not overstay your welcome.

So, now that you know what to expect, how do you go about meeting one of those 333 million Americans? As we've seen, Americans are doers, joiners, and organizers. They can't resist talking to someone who shares their particular passion, so whatever your professional or leisure interest, find a group and get involved. A nation of networkers, Americans will generously extend introductions and make connections for you. Mention that you like to hike and someone will introduce you to their coworker's cousin's wife who knows all the best trails. Bars and parties can be hit or miss in terms of meeting like-minded people, but if nothing else provide a fun night out.

After initial introductions, it may be assumed that you're doing okay or are happy to fend for yourself. Remember that Americans respect independence and privacy. But if you do reach out, you'll be met with generous offers of advice or help. If a commitment to friendship is made, Americans will sweep you off your feet with unparalleled enthusiasm and generosity.

GREETINGS

The customary greeting is "Hi. How are you?" accompanied by a smile and an out-thrust hand. You're not expected to provide a detailed report on the state of your health. A similarly vague, upbeat "Fine. How are you?" is appropriate. When being introduced to other guests, first and last names are presented, which is an invitation to continue on a first-name basis. Titles are reserved for professional situations. Students used to call teachers, neighbors, and family friends by the last name—and even "Sir" and "Ma'am"—but this practice is being relaxed, although it may still be followed in parts of the "gracious South."

People are expected to mingle and introduce themselves to each other. Americans generally have polished social skills and exude self-confidence. They're good at remembering your name—or what they think is your name. Nobody would expect you to memorize a lineup of strangers, however, so don't be afraid to ask someone to repeat their name. It'll help you remember, and it's often a good opening for small talk.

COME ON OVER!

Once an invitation is forthcoming, relax and enjoy it. American hospitality is legendary. Dinner may be a formal, three-course affair on fine china or a buffet on a paper plate. Informality rules and everyone pitches in. It's polite when invited to ask if you can bring something. Your offer may be politely declined, although close friends may be asked to bring a salad or dessert. (But don't turn up empty-handed—a well-chosen bottle of wine or a small bunch of flowers are generally acceptable. See "Gifts," opposite.) At a potluck dinner everyone is assigned a dish to prepare to share the load. (Insider tip: offering to bring wine can be a preemptive strike if you struggle to make a five-bean salad.)

Apartment dwellers with tiny kitchens may prefer to take you out to a restaurant. If it isn't clear that you're a guest, be prepared to pay your share of the bill when it arrives—your hosts will quickly clarify the situation. You can still offer to pay the tip, but if you're being treated, just accept with thanks.

Holiday entertaining such as at Christmas or Thanksgiving is family style, with guests serving themselves from platters of food that are handed around the table. Cocktail parties are a popular way of introducing a large number of people to each other—parents at the beginning of the school year, for instance, newcomers to the neighborhood, or a get-together before a conference. (If the occasion is "official," there's no need to bring a gift.)

No one stands on ceremony. The greatest honor is not to be waited upon, but to be included and told to "help yourself" and "make yourself at home." The enjoyment is in the pleasure of each other's company—not in the perfection of the meal or the service.

For a formal dinner, arrive within fifteen minutes of the indicated time; for a party, up to thirty minutes is fine. Just don't arrive early or precisely on time. (Unless you're invited to a concert or a play, when it's essential to be early.) Unlike other social events, cocktail party invitations stipulate an end as well as a start time, which should be observed.

Dress code is usually smart casual unless an invitation stipulates otherwise. For barbecues or picnics, take it down another notch and break out the shorts and sandals. If you're unsure, it's okay to ask your host ahead of time.

Let's Do Lunch!

A recently arrived expatriate, Beth, was concerned. Everyone she met ended the conversation with "let's do lunch," but no one had called. Beth hadn't committed any terrible cultural faux pas. Like many visitors, she had misinterpreted the warm, open American communication style for an indication of friendship. While her colleagues were demonstrating genuine interest and good intentions, the reality is that tight schedules may prevent people from following up. "We must get together" may not be an invitation but a polite way to bring closure to a conversation.

Gifts

If invited for dinner, you can't go wrong with flowers, candy, or a bottle of wine (as long as your hosts imbibe). If you're a weekend houseguest, a "hostess gift"—a small decorative object or book—is appropriate. You can also offer to take your hosts to lunch or dinner during your stay, but don't be surprised if it doesn't fit their timetable.

CHAPTER FIVE

AT HOME

AMERICA'S HOMES, SWEET HOMES

In the pioneering days, when the government was offering free land, legend has it that settlers would gallop into the dusty interior and stick a stake in the ground to claim ownership. Americans today may keep one eye on the mortgage rates before "plotting their stake" into a California subdivision—but despite the ever-increasing cost of getting a foothold in the housing market, home ownership remains a big part of the American Dream.

Early American housing reflected the local climate and available materials. Spanish colonists in the Southwest (inspired by Native American structures) built adobe dwellings; New Englanders constructed gabled houses of local wood; wealthy nineteenth-century industrialists favored European stone and marble. The South is an architectural historian's paradise. From the ornate iron balconies of the French quarter in New Orleans to the Spanish antebellum mansions of Mississippi and Georgia, or the sprawling Texan ranch, each is an exercise in adapting imported ethnic influences to the demands of the local terrain and lifestyle.

Today, America has its share of subdivisions—housing developments featuring identical homes on well-manicured adjoining plots. Wherever possible, however, styles of homes are expressions of American individuality. A stroll through a suburban neighborhood might reveal a columned Greek revival style sandwiched between a colonial farmhouse and an English Tudor-style property. None may be more than two years old! And most will be constructed from wood, in plentiful supply across the nation. The current choice of builders is the super-sized "McMansion," a plot-bursting house that gives everybody in the family space to hide from each other while they surf the net or tweet their passing thoughts.

Inspired by the wanderlust of their predecessors, Americans move around the country, for college, for work, or just for a change of lifestyle. The average American moves about twelve times in his or her lifetime. (For comparison, the average is only four times in Europe, and the average Brit moves once every twenty-three years.)

In terms of domestic migration trends, the population is becoming increasingly urbanized. A nation of farmers no more, only one in five live in rural America, which covers 97 percent of the land area. The Northeast is losing population while the suburbs of the South continue to gain. In the 2020 census, for example, the biggest winners were Phoenix in Arizona; Houston, Dallas, and Austin in Texas; and Atlanta in Georgia, while New York City shrunk.

Iconic brownstone houses in New York.

City living is characterized by socioeconomic extremes. In New York City, for instance, government-subsidized, low-income housing projects and lavish multimillion-dollar condos coexist on neighboring blocks. Older style housing consists of row houses—townhouses or "brownstones" (named for the color of the local stone used for their façades) of three to four stories, attached on both sides. They may be single-family dwellings or divided into smaller apartments or studios. Some high-rise apartment buildings have a population the size of a small village.

In contrast, the suburbs are the bastion of the manicured "yard" (garden), basketball hoop, pool, and minivan. In the warmer, Southern states, smaller condo complexes with communal facilities are popular with retirees and single professionals alike. The rise of "gated communities" reflects a desire for security, convenience, and the instant sense of community that's difficult for the transient American to achieve.

The recent "cocooning" trend, encouraged by Web sites and TV channels devoted to home decoration and real estate, was already leading Americans to invest more time and money than ever in their homes, even before Covid trapped them there for a while. The do-it-yourself mentality has spawned a huge industry of books, TV programs, and hangar-sized home improvement stores for the "weekend warrior," hoisting sheetrock onto the roof of his SUV. Satisfaction is gained as much from the process as the end product. A "fixer-upper" house will be transformed into a dream home—then the owners will move on, ready for the next project.

Don't Fence Me In

The issue of privacy versus openness is a paradox— particularly when it comes to the American home. "Lots" or "yards" can be large, and many are not enclosed by the walls, fences, or hedges so prevalent in other cultures. Indoors, the use of European-style net curtains to screen out nosey neighbors is rare. In the same vein, first-time visitors to an American home may be proudly given the full tour; even walk-in closets and en suite bathrooms aren't considered off-limits. They may also be encouraged to help themselves to a soda from the fridge. All this gives an impression of openness.

Yet Americans do value their personal space and privacy. While a typical suburban home features spacious, communal areas, such as an open-plan kitchen and family room or "den," ample private space is also allowed in the floor plan. A visit to a family home in the evening would likely find the family members dispersed, each independently watching TV, chatting online with friends, or surfing the net—and possibly all three at the same time—in the privacy of their own bedroom.

A common observation is just how outsized everything is. The beds are king-sized, the home theater TVs have giant screens and multi-speaker sound systems, the burgers are "whoppers," appliances are "industrial" size. The largest popcorn or soda at the movies can be "supersized." Closets are "walk-in," and some cars are the size of a military vehicle. But again, there are some signs of a backlash among motorists, driven by environmental issues and soaring prices at the gas pumps—Hummers are out, hybrids and Teslas are in.

THE BLENDED FAMILY

What does an American family look like? A mosaic that slowly but constantly shifts as demographic patterns and attitudes change.

Couples are getting married later (median age thirty for a man and twenty-eight for a woman), if at all. The numbers are dropping from state to state, but nearly half of all first marriages end in divorce. This is probably why more couples prefer to live together without taking the trip down the aisle. In the 2020 census, fewer than half of US households were married couples, with or without children. Young people are also increasingly likely to live with their parents into their twenties and thirties.

Advances in medical technology are allowing women to have children later. More than half of the births to American mothers younger than thirty are outside marriage. One in three Americans is a "step" relative, whether it's a parent, sibling, or child. And thanks to notable Supreme Court decisions, same-sex couples can now marry and adopt children in all states.

America's birthrate continues to decline, while life expectancy has increased. By the year 2030 it's estimated that one in five Americans will be over the age of sixty-five. This means that Generation X and Millennials have to care and plan simultaneously for parents and children.

In families with two parents, gender equality has reached the boardroom—and the kitchen. The number of dual-earner couples outnumbers the "breadwinner/homemaker"

combo by three to one, and in the latter case, that homemaker is increasingly likely to be a stay-at-home dad.

Despite these trends, surveys show that most Americans still consider family to be the ideal and the bedrock of society. So how has society coped with the seismic shifts of the twenty-first century? Americans have risen to the challenge with their customary tolerance, adaptability, and resourcefulness, particularly during the first years of the Covid-19 pandemic. Creative solutions involving alliances of grandparents, stepparents, single parents, and babysitters make complex family situations work. Statistics show that the combination of smaller families and labor-saving devices means that while working parents may be guilt-ridden, they actually have more time available to spend with their children than any generation before them.

GROWING UP IN THE USA

Visitors from cultures where children are raised to be seen but not heard can be shocked at the amount of consultation and negotiation between American parents and their children. The American family is a democracy. Relatively young children are included in family decisions—from choosing burgers or spaghetti for lunch to Florida or California for vacation. Youngsters will usually dictate what they eat, wear, and how they spend their time at an earlier age than in other societies.

Everyone has a right to be heard—no matter how young. This means that parents can be interrupted or a teacher's statement challenged. Such behavior would be deemed disrespectful in a more hierarchical society. To individualistic Americans it's a simple matter of expressing an opinion, being an active learner, and exercising their rights. Authority figures don't merit automatic deference, but should earn respect through their actions. Teachers shouldn't be placed on a pedestal, but rather be partners in learning. And parents should be able to answer the question "but why?" rationally. When it comes to discipline, physically reprimanding a child with a smack is severely frowned upon. Parents encourage children to mediate the sandbox skirmishes for themselves. "Use your words," they're taught.

Both the educational system and home life instill the values of independence, self-reliance, and self-expression. This ethos is first displayed in kindergarten in "show and tell," where children build confidence and self-esteem by talking about an interest or achievement to classmates. Rather than rote learning, the emphasis is on teaching educational self-sufficiency through research, analysis, and problem-solving skills. A percentage of class grade, from first grade to graduate school, is based on class participation, rewarding students for speaking up and "making their mark."

Independence is learned in a series of time-honored steps, as responsibility is gradually meted out. Children as young as six will go on "sleepovers" at each other's houses. Schools and civic and private organizations provide many outward-bound activities. The ultimate sign of independence is "getting wheels." In many states, teens can drive at sixteen or seventeen. Driving is considered so important that many schools offer "driver education."

Outsiders who judge American society based on media images may be critical of the amount of freedom given to teens. The philosophy is to empower the individual by preparing them with practical information and a sense of moral responsibility. Rather than shielding children from the world, it allows them to take risks. The greatest learning, after all, comes from one's mistakes.

Schools play their part, usually providing a comprehensive education program that incorporates civic responsibility. In the light of tragic school shootings often perpetrated by youngsters who "didn't fit in," there's a greater sensitivity to peer pressure, bullying, and the cliquish nature of larger high schools, where "nerds," "goths," "emos," "geeks," and "jocks" are powerful subcultures. Sadly, social networking can now make "cyberbullying" a 24-hour activity. Every kid now has a camera-equipped smartphone to instantly share their school friends' moments of triumph and embarrassment with the world.

Making the Grade

Americans often assume their way is the world's way. (They're often right.) So if you ask how old a child is, you'll probably just be told their "grade" in the US educational system, which isn't the alphabetic grade that's a score of academic achievement. It gets even more confusing when the answer is that someone's teenage son or daughter is a "junior" or a "sophomore."

As a rule of thumb, add five to the grade to get the child's approximate age. (But you may occasionally hear of a child who's been "held back a grade"—made to repeat a year—to improve his or her academic performance.) Below is a basic guide to grades—the numerical kind.

GRADE	CHILD'S AGE AT START OF SCHOOL YEAR
ELEMENTARY SCHOOL	
Kindergarten	5
First	6
Second	7
Third	8
Fourth	9
Fifth	10
MIDDLE SCHOOL	
Sixth	11
Seventh	12
Eighth	13
HIGH SCHOOL	
Ninth or "Freshman"*	14
Tenth or "Sophomore"*	15
Eleventh or "Junior"*	16
Twelfth or "Senior"*	17

*These terms are used over again for the four years of "junior" college. This may typically begin at age eighteen, but some students take a break of a year or two between high school and college.

Yale University campus, New Haven, Conneticut.

EDUCATION

Like many other aspects of American life, the people
refuse to let the government control education.
Expatriate families are often shocked to discover that
there's no national education system. Most school
funding is at the state level, and each district has an
elected board of education to set the curriculum and
handle administration. Standards vary so widely that the

quality of local schooling often determines where families choose to live. School boards can sometimes be controlled by a group with an agenda, such as forcing the science-lite Intelligent Design into the curriculum, banning books from the library, or sidestepping any mention of LGBTQ families or the troubling truth about slavery. Even today, American classics such as *Huckleberry Finn* or *To Kill a Mockingbird* are challenged for their racial content. Some boards believe the Harry Potter series promotes witchcraft.

While the vast majority of children attend public (state-run) schools, many parents look to alternative options, such as independent (private) schools or home schooling. There are also schools with religious affiliations, such as Jewish or Catholic parochial schools, where students can receive the religious instruction forbidden in public schools.

Extracurricular activities are considered an integral part of a child's overall education. Through participation in music, sports, science, arts, and community-service activities, children broaden their horizons and learn new skills.

Similarly, the work ethic kicks in early. With that first roadside lemonade stand, American children of all backgrounds get a taste for financial independence. This often starts with them doing basic household chores in exchange for an allowance (pocket money), continues in the form of a "paper route" or babysitting job, and progresses to weekend work at a local store or restaurant.

Some claim that all these activities lead to stressed-out families and children who are too tightly scheduled. On the whole, however, American children seem to thrive by keeping busy and are often well prepared to meet the demands and responsibilities of adult life.

Higher Education

A combination of government loans, scholarships, and grants, together with various means of practical support, encourages students from all walks of life to continue their studies. Indeed, America boasts a higher proportion of higher education students than any other country. In 2022 close to half of eighteen to twenty-four-year-olds were in college. Approximately one in three adults over twenty-five had an undergraduate degree (a bachelor's or the two-year associate's degree), while 13 percent had graduate degrees—a master's or better.

The system focuses on breadth rather than depth of education, with students not selecting a "major" field of study until as late as the third year of a four-year bachelor's degree.

American education is also characterized by its flexibility—course credits earned can be switched to a different college, or applied to a different major.

Back to School

"College," "University," even "School," are terms used somewhat interchangeably.

So why does a country that spends more than most industrialized nations on education trail world rankings in academic achievement tests? The answer may lie in its heterogeneity and the sheer numbers that pass through the system. Educators would also point out that real specialization in the USA is only expected at the postgraduate level. America is home to many of the world's most prestigious graduate schools, where it takes another two to three years to gain a master's, and up to eight for a doctorate.

When a third of the population has an undergraduate degree, some further differentiation is required. That's when the status of the college or university where that degree was earned comes into play. A degree from one of the eight "Ivy League" (private) universities may be considered a passport for life. But many other schools are highly prestigious, and an American will name-drop his or her alma mater with pride, perhaps assuming its reputation and "personality" are widely known (even though the overseas visitor may have heard only of Harvard and Yale). Another distinctive feature of the education system is the high cost of tuition. Of America's nearly 4,000 higher education institutions, approximately half are private (as opposed to state-owned "public" universities, many of which have outstanding reputations).

The pursuit of excellence comes at a cost. According to official figures, in 2022 an education on a "moderate" budget at a public university cost about $35,000 per year (tuition, fees, and daily living expenses), rising to about

$53,000 per year at a private college. This explains why many families start saving for college before Junior has uttered his or her first word. Many students have to be self-supporting, working their way through college, or taking out a student loan. This means that many graduate with a degree—and a heavy debt burden. Pile in the loss of potential job income during those college years plus interest on student loans, and it's estimated that a bachelor's degree can cost more than $400,000.

THE DAILY GRIND

Just as there are many family structures, so there are a range of work arrangements. For some, the daily commute involves an hour in bumper-to-bumper traffic. For "telecommuters," it means navigating the kids' toys to get from the kitchen to the home office. Companies eager to retain high-performing employees are offering on-site childcare facilities, flexible schedules, and paternity leave. As a result of the coronavirus pandemic, many companies now also offer employees flexible work-from-home options.

Before Covid-19 hit, nearly 60 percent of women were working—they generally make up more than half the work force—although those who choose to be stay-at-home moms are likely to be equally busy, juggling carpooling, community volunteering, further education, exercising, home improvement projects, and countless other activities. During the pandemic, more women than

Morning commuters on their way to work, Chicago, Illinois.

men gave up their jobs and once lockdowns were over were slower to return to work, largely due to an increase in childcare responsibilities.

Meals are often eaten on the run—at the desk, in the car, or in front of the laptop. Dinner time may be the only opportunity for families to gather and catch up on the day's events. Discussions may range from world news to the status of a homework project. The food may be take-out Chinese or Italian, something from the freezer, or a home-cooked dinner.

Time is precious, the day is tightly scheduled, and disruptions are unwelcome. Friends and family usually call first before dropping by, and calls and texts may be screened. As email, texting, and voicemail blur the lines further between work and leisure time, evenings are often spent on the phone or computer, or figuring out what needs to be added to tomorrow's to-do list. Ubiquitous smartphones—by 2022, close to 90 percent of Americans had at least one device—means every household now has access to the online world.

For convenience, grocery shopping is often done in bulk on a weekly basis at large supermarkets. The newcomer will be either amused or overwhelmed by the amount of choice, with entire aisles devoted to breakfast cereals or pasta sauce. Store hours vary enormously. Smaller stores open from 9:00 a.m. to 6:00 p.m. Suburban supermarkets often stay open till 8:00 or 9:00 p.m. Some convenience stores (often attached to gas stations) stay open until midnight. In large cities, corner delis and some supermarkets operate around the clock. About 10 percent of shoppers prefer to avoid the hassle of going to the store and order their groceries online instead, for home delivery or in-store pick-up. That's expected to double by 2026.

CHAPTER SIX

TIME OUT

Americans work hard and play hard. They may exchange the trading floor for the gym or garden, but they approach their leisure time with the same energy and single-mindedness they apply to the workday. "Thank God it's Friday" means packing as much into the weekend as possible!

A snapshot of a typical suburban Saturday morning would reveal cars being washed, lawns mown, and home projects tackled. Media images may portray Americans as either sedentary couch potatoes or Lycra-clad extreme athletes, but most fall comfortably in the middle. The great outdoors is America's playground. Even the workaholic will make time to play golf, hike, cycle, or ski. Excellent community facilities and subsidized programs mean that, compared with other countries, a wide range of recreational activities are accessible to most people. Closer to home, there are farmers' markets to visit, garage sales to browse, antique stores to explore, and get-togethers to organize.

For a nation of individualists, Americans are also "joiners." Although watching TV is still the number one pastime, six out of ten belong to at least one club. This may be a local civic group, such as the Rotary Club or Lions, a special interest group, or a sports club. If Junior is playing Little League baseball, Dad—or Mom—is as likely to be coaching as watching.

VACATIONS

Many Americans get just two weeks' annual vacation. This may be supplemented by long-weekend getaways, slotted around public holidays, but it still means that even vacations are enjoyed at a frenetic pace, especially since more Americans are venturing beyond the continental edges. In contrast, school summer holidays have always been ten to twelve weeks long, the tradition originating in the need for children to help out on the family farm. Not many sixth graders have to pitch in with the harvest these days, so working parents are thankful for the range of local programs/activities and "sleepaway" camps to keep children busy and develop their rugged independence.

SHOP TILL THEY DROP

Americans have always loved to shop. How does one account for the staggering amount of consumerism in the United States? Is it the deserved fruits of one's labors, or economic one-upmanship in a classless society? It may simply be that because consumer goods are so cheap, it makes more sense to replace that burned-out hairdryer than get it fixed, leading to the perception of a disposable society. Transience in trends, reflecting the desire for constant change, means many Americans will buy today's look and replace it in a couple of years.

Various items that are regarded as luxuries elsewhere are, in the States, considered essential to sustaining the way of life. That second car provides transport to work. Everyone can retreat to their own bedroom with a laptop, a smartphone, and maybe an iPad too. A combination of high labor costs and the desire for privacy leads people to invest in labor-saving devices over household help. These in turn free up time and energy for more worthwhile pursuits. Americans know there will always be a way to pay. "Plastic meltdown" (credit-card debt) doesn't have the same stigma it has in other societies.

Shopping is easy. Keep the receipt to exchange goods or get a refund, no questions asked. Before you count out exact change, remember that in most states a sales tax (as high as 7.25 percent in California, down to nothing in Alaska, Delaware, Montana, New Hampshire, and Oregon) will be added on to many items at the checkout. Sales are held on practically every holiday weekend at department stores.

The mall is the epicenter of suburban life. Here, families shop, eat, and go to the movies. Teens work part-time or simply gather and hang out. Grandma and her buddies may even power walk around the many safe, undercover miles it provides.

Will it continue? More than 75 percent of Americans regularly buy online these days. But ecommerce—people's number one online activity, creeping toward revenue of a trillion dollars a year—still doesn't account for more than 20 percent of all US spending. Buyers like to touch, feel, and maybe try on a potential purchase before they lay down the dollars. Many Americans will check out an item on their smartphones or laptops, but then make the expedition to a brick-and-mortar store to bring it home.

HOW TO PAY

Credit and debit cards—essential for making hotel and car rental reservations—are widely accepted across America. Visa, Mastercard, and American Express are generally the traveler's best bet. Most purchases can now be made via contactless payment, with a wave of your card or through your smartphone, even in New York taxis. Prepaid cards are also available at some banks, but may cost you more. Travelers' checks are fast becoming antiquated.

If you need cash, say for tips, ATMs can be found on almost every city street corner, and most accept foreign-issued bank cards. Be careful with those banknotes. American bills are all the same size and colors, so take a good look at the value before you hand it over.

SPORTS—PLAY BALL!

Sports in America is about seven-year-olds learning "team spirit" from the neighborhood Little League coach. It's also about big business. Top universities compete for sporting preeminence as well as scholastic achievement. Scouts are dispatched to watch promising high-school students, who may be offered college sports scholarships worth thousands of dollars. At the professional level, players' salaries reach into the stratosphere. The lines between sport and business are further blurred as the competitive language of sport and business jargon become ever more interchangeable. Players who reach their sport's "Hall of Fame" are revered for life and are as well known inside America as movie stars.

Americans love their homegrown sports and all the nostalgia, rituals, and sideshow entertainment that accompany them. No real work is done at the office until the "Monday morning quarterback sessions" (postgame analyses) have taken place. At professional or college level, in stadiums or on TV, America's top three sports—basketball, football, and baseball—draw huge numbers. Soccer, hockey (in America, that's always ice hockey), and NASCAR—stock car racing—come next in popularity. Americans may stray from their roots, but they always stay true to their hometown sports team.

The rules of each game are too complex to explain here. However, the sports-mad American will be only too happy to explain a game's intricacies at the ballpark or sports bar.

Baseball

Baseball is affectionately referred to as "the national pastime." It has also been described as the most

A view from the grandstands at Dodger Stadium, Los Angeles.

democratic of sports, played by men of all heights and weights. The formfitting uniforms, some with distinctive pinstripes, can't conceal the odd paunch, but don't try telling Americans that their "boys of summer" aren't athletes.

The Major League teams—the "majors"—are split into two leagues, the American League and the National League, with fifteen teams in each. During the April-to-October season, they compete within their leagues and then, in "post-season" play, the teams with the best record compete for their league championship, or "pennant." The two winners meet in the best-of-seven-games World Series. ("World"? Well, there's one Canadian team left in the majors, the Toronto Blue Jays, after the Montreal Expos defected to Washington in 2005.)

Baseball evokes nostalgia like no other sport—just ask an octogenarian Brooklynite about the childhood trauma of being told his beloved Dodgers were relocating to LA. For spectators, baseball is a participation sport, punctuated by traditions such as the "seventh inning stretch," the ritual singing of "Take Me Out to the Ball Game," and the consumption of beer, pretzels, and "crackerjack."

Basketball

Basketball started in 1891 when James Naismith, a minister, seeking a new game for boisterous YMCA youths, nailed a peach net on to a gymnasium wall. Today it's the only American sport to have been exported successfully around the world. Visitors will hear the sound of a bouncing basketball everywhere in the States. Friends are made over "pick up" games on public courts; teens "shoot hoops" in suburban driveways, and dream of becoming the next LeBron James.

The National Basketball Association (NBA) was originally formed in 1946. The season runs from September to April. There are thirty professional teams,

Friends play basketball in Scotia, New York.

divided into two "conferences." Playoffs are held in April and May, when the best eight teams in each group vie for conference championship, and then the two ultimate winners meet in the NBA World Championship in June. ("World"? Yes, there's one Canadian basketball team, too.)

The National Collegiate Athletic Association (NCAA) features 358 teams and has a passionate following, rivaling that of the professional league. The college season climaxes when 68 teams compete to win the "March Madness" tournament.

The Women's National Basketball Association (WNBA) was created in 1996 and now features twelve professional teams. The popular All-Star Game takes place in July, and the season wraps up with playoffs in September leading to the best-of-five finals between the two top teams in October.

Football

American football—which is not soccer—was adapted from the English game of rugby. First played at the college level in the late 1800s, it was deemed so brutal that President Theodore Roosevelt insisted the game be made safer. Today, despite the full armor of helmets and padding, the game is as much about speed and strategy as strength.

The National Football League (NFL) divides its thirty-two teams into two "conferences." The seventeen-game season usually runs from September to December, and the best six in each conference then take part in the playoffs in January, with the two ultimate champions battling for final supremacy in the "Super Bowl." (No "World"? Nope, no Canadian team.)

"Superbowl Sunday" in late January or early February is arguably the sports highlight of the year. The championship final tops the TV ratings, as much for its humorous beer commercials and half-time extravaganza as for the game itself. The nation stops, friends gather, and sales in chips and dip skyrocket.

The highlights of the fall college football season are the various "bowl games" played between the champions of the different college leagues, the "Rose Bowl" in Pasadena being the biggest.

Jets, Mets, or Nets?

In baseball, basketball, football, and hockey, team names include its current home—the NBA's Miami Heat, the NFL's Dallas Cowboys—but sports fans and announcers alike tend to drop the location and just talk about "the Braves" or "the Lakers." For example, Detroit fields the Tigers for baseball, the Pistons for basketball, the Lions for football, and the Red Wings for hockey. You'd have more work to do in New York, which supports two teams in each of those sports, plus a women's basketball team. (Three of those nine teams are named in the header.)

To confuse the issue, scoreboards show only the city name. And some teams pick up other nicknames—in baseball, the New York Yankees, or Yanks, masquerade as the "Bronx Bombers," the Oakland Athletics are always "the A's."

Soccer

Even though it's not a homegrown sport, professional soccer has caught on big time, and it's crept up to fourth place in popularity (third place if you're just watching it). Kids played the game for years, first kicking a ball around a playground, then in Saturday-morning leagues and summer camps. Now Major League Soccer (MLS) fields twenty-five men's professional teams from the USA (plus three from Canada), while there are twelve teams in the current National Women's Soccer League (NWSL).

Despite hosting the 1994 FIFA World Cup, the US men's national team has yet to make a major impact on the global soccer scene. Not so the women, whose four World Cup triumphs since 1991 and four Olympic gold medals put them well ahead of any other international side.

OTHER HIGHLIGHTS OF THE SPORTING CALENDAR

National Ice Hockey League—season starts in October and culminates in the late May/early June Stanley Cup Championship

US Open Golf—mid-June

US Open Tennis—late August/early September

The Kentucky Derby (horse race)—first Saturday in May

NASCAR stock car racing—including the Daytona 500 (February) and Indianapolis 500 (May)

EATING OUT

Americans will find any excuse to eat out—to socialize, for convenience, or simply for the excellent value offered by those huge breakfasts, "early bird" specials, and all-you-can-eat buffets.

Fast food aside, it's difficult to think of an American national dish, although comfort foods such as chicken pot pie, mac and cheese, and meatloaf probably come close. Many popular foods have been Americanized from the national cuisines of immigrants.

One can probably find the most authentic American food at the regional level, and the most intriguing names—bear claw, popover, jerky, or gumbo, anyone? Southern cuisine is influenced by its French, African-American, and Mexican heritage. "Soul foods" include chicken-fried steak, biscuits and gravy, ham-hock stew, and collard greens. Louisiana is home to Creole and Cajun-style cooking. Local favorites are crawfish bisque, blackened catfish, and jambalaya (rice with ham, sausage, and shrimp). Mexican enchiladas, burritos, fajitas, and salsas have been enthusiastically embraced north of the border.

Midwestern European imports are evident in the Scandinavian fish boils, Polish pierogis, and German bratwurst. In the Northeast, many ethnic foods have become mainstream. At New York street fairs neighboring stalls sell Jewish knishes, Greek spinach pastries, and Italian ziti and cannoli. This region also offers the best of indigenous produce—maple syrup, turkey, corn, pumpkin—not to mention the world-class lobster and Baltimore crab cakes.

From the top: spicy Cajun jambalaya with sausage and shrimp; Southern-style collard greens and bacon; Jewish potato dumpling knishes.

On the other side of the country, east meets west to create fusion cuisine—Pacific salmon served on a bed of Mexican salsa, or Montana beef tossed in a wok with Asian noodles and vegetables.

Even for simple meals, such as breakfast or a quick lunch, the decisions to be made when ordering can seem interminable. Do you prefer 1 percent or 2 percent fat milk in your coffee? Or perhaps soy milk, oat milk, almond milk, cream, or "half and half" (half milk, half cream). Then there are the ten different ways of preparing eggs, an impossible variety of sandwich breads, and a bewildering selection of salad dressings to choose from. It may seem redundant to ask for "lite" maple syrup to accompany that towering stack of pancakes, yet people do.

The Barbecue Wars

A "cookout" is simply an alternative name for a barbecue. A "cook-off," on the other hand, is an annual contest featuring chefs from Texas, South Carolina, and Kentucky, vying to assert their state's supremacy in the barbecue wars.

You Want Fries with That?

One aspect of American life that needs no instruction is fast food—the hamburger and its cousins. You've seen them in your hometown. There's not much difference on their home turf, and that's a deliberate corporate policy.

But as Americans are invited to "supersize" their precooked lunches (and often breakfasts and dinners as well), they're also supersizing themselves. Those cheap, convenient, low-cost, low-nutrition, high-fat, high-calorie, so-called meals have led to a society where obesity is a significant health problem, although other contributors are "activities" that don't involve getting up from the sofa and vast drinks that are little more than sugar solutions. Obesity among children has tripled in a generation. One in six children is seriously overweight.

Coffee Culture

Americans have always preferred coffee to tea, but credit for raising the simple act of ordering a cup of coffee to a degree-level subject must go to a certain Seattle chain. Many use their local Starbucks or similar as a "virtual office," holding everything from meetings to interviews there, their laptops firmly plugged in next to their lattes.

Tea Drinkers Beware

If you order tea anywhere but in the most sophisticated establishments, you'll be unceremoniously served a cup of hot (but nowhere near boiling) water with a teabag and a stirrer, plus a carton or two of the creamy "half-and-half"—that is, unless you're in the South, in which case you'll be asked if you want "sweet tea," which is iced tea with sugar added. (A top tip: that "hot" water is often nowhere near hot enough for black tea, but it's not a bad temperature for making green tea.)

"One for the Road"

American bars take many forms, yet they aren't, as a rule, the social equivalents of the family friendly continental café or the British local pub. American ads may boast that water from the Rocky Mountains gives their beer its distinctive taste; visitors often claim they add a little too much of the stuff, making American beer weaker than its European counterparts. For beer connoisseurs, however, there are ample alternatives in the vast range of microbrewery and imported bottled beers. And, of course, the soils of California and Oregon produce world-class wines. Many bars feature a "happy hour" early in the evening, with heavily discounted drinks. It's customary to leave a small tip ($1) for the bartender on the bar with each round of drinks.

Laws regulating the sale of liquor vary from state to state. In most states, the minimum drinking age is twenty-one and before entering an establishment where liquor is sold, patrons will be asked for a photo ID card (usually a driver's license) to prove their date of birth.

BARTENDER!

Straight up—without water or ice

On the rocks—with ice

With a twist—with a piece of lemon

Salt or not salt around the rim—state your preference when ordering a margarita

Dining Etiquette

There are few hard and fast rules of dining etiquette in this relaxed culture. When a group of friends dine out together, they usually "go Dutch," dividing the bill equally among the number of guests. Don't forget to add at least a 15 percent tip (see opposite).

Americans generally cut their food with the knife in the right hand, and then switch the knife and fork. The knife is placed on the plate, and the bite-sized food is eaten with the fork in the right hand.

A lot of food is eaten with the hands—fried chicken, French fries, hamburgers, and tacos, for instance—which is probably why napkins are used at even the most informal meals. Portions are huge, and at all but the most sophisticated restaurants it is acceptable to ask for a "doggie bag" for leftovers. These days no one even tries to pretend that the seafood risotto is really for Fido.

WHEN ORDERING

A la mode—A scoop of ice cream added to pie.

PBJ—A peanut butter and jelly sandwich. America's favorite. (It's usually grape jelly.)

BLT—Bacon, lettuce, and tomato sandwich.

Hero—A long (a foot or more), overstuffed bread roll. (Alt. sub, short for submarine)

Soda—A generic term for any carbonated drink, such as Coke or 7-Up. But a "club soda" is carbonated water, as is a "seltzer." (The difference? Club soda has salt.)

Sunny-side up—A regular fried egg.

Once over easy—An egg that's fried on both sides.

TIPPING
....

Visitors should be aware that many workers in service industries receive the minimum wage and rely on tips to make a decent income. The expected amount varies, but it's more in tourist areas, larger cities, and better-class hotels, restaurants, or hair salons.

As a general rule, add 15 percent to a taxi fare. Hairdressers expect 10 to 15 percent. Allow $1 a bag for bellhops and airport porters (more if you're toting a trunk full of college books or an unwieldy ski bag).

A standard tip in a restaurant would be 15 percent—less if you sit at a diner's counter— and up to 20 percent in a good restaurant for excellent service.

As the state tax added to the bill is often in the region of 8 percent, many Americans simply double the tax to calculate the tip. This means that diners should estimate paying 25 percent above the actual price of a meal to include both the tip and the tax.

The Evil Weed …

Smoky jazz bars are a thing of the past. Movie houses, theaters, buses, trains, and airplanes banned tobacco use years ago, and now nearly half of all Americans live in a city where smoking isn't permitted in the workplace, in bars, or in restaurants. (Most Americans live where at least one of these bans applies.) State law applies, with community variations and additions. If you're a smoker, you'd better check the local regulations, and obey all posted signs. And don't think you can get away with just lighting up a cigarette and hoping nobody will say anything. They will.

… and the Legal Weed

The majority of states have legalized marijuana, at least for medicinal use and increasingly for recreation, too. More than one in three adults over 21 are already regular users, and two-thirds of Americans say they want the federal government to follow through and legalize pot at the national level. Until then, check before you toke or vape or scarf down that hash brownie—and note that restrictions on where you can smoke apply whatever you're puffing. Don't drive high!

CULTURE

For a long while, Americans imported their high culture from Europe. It wasn't until the nineteenth century that the country took its indigenous art forms seriously. Fusing the influences and experiences of its people, it has stamped its own, singularly American style on the world of art and culture. The USA is home to some of the world's best museums and galleries, but the visitor should also explore America's homegrown contributions to the creative arts.

America excels at making culture more democratic and less stuffy. While some Americans still get decked out in their finery for the opera, casual dress is the norm at the theater. You'll see everything from cocktail dresses to shorts and sandals.

Certainly, a subscription to the opera or symphony might be expensive, but you can always attend the many free outdoor events or the affordable regional or experimental theater productions. There's something for every taste and budget. When it comes to tickets, local knowledge can save big bucks, so check with a friend or the hotel concierge to get the inside scoop on discounted tickets. Big cities may have places where you can buy unsold tickets for same-day performances, such as the TKTS booth in New York's Times Square, which also has its own app where you can see what's available.

Theater

American playwrights have tackled the country's social issues head on, entertaining and moving generations of audiences. Notable authors include Arthur Miller, Eugene O'Neill, Tennessee Williams, Edward Albee, David Mamet, August Wilson, Tony Kushner, and John Guare. New York City's "Broadway"—around Times Square—is the nation's center for drama and musicals, but all major cities have their own theater scene.

Musical Theater

The equivalent of Britain's music hall, the variety acts of America's vaudeville were developed into the Broadway musical. The classic shows, including *Showboat*, *Carousel*, and *Forty-Second Street*, are regularly revived. Irving Berlin, Cole Porter, and Frank Loesser incorporated American themes, humor, and pathos in their offerings—all sandwiched between high-kicking, show-stopping numbers. The musicals of Richard Rodgers and Lorenz Hart dominated the Broadway stage (and Hollywood) for the first half of the twentieth century, but when Rodgers paired with lyricist Oscar Hammerstein to write *Oklahoma* in 1948, it paved the way for productions where song and dance no longer "stopped the show" but propelled the story forward. The immortal genius Stephen Sondheim (*Company*, *Sweeney Todd*) supplied both the music and lyrics for haunting, uncompromising musicals that defy categorization. In recent years, musical transformations of Disney movies and other silver screen successes have featured on Broadway, including many with music by Alan Menken.

"Off Broadway"

In New York, the designations "off Broadway" and "off off Broadway" don't refer to proximity to the "Great White Way," but rather the size of the theater. However, this can be an indication of the type of show. Lavish musicals fill the larger Broadway theaters, straight plays tend to occupy off-Broadway venues, while the more intimate off-off-Broadway theaters are home to exciting experimental works.

The popular concert venue Carnegie Hall in Midtown Manhattan, New York.

Opera and Symphony

Thanks to private philanthropy, most cities have their own symphony orchestra and several also boast an opera company. A recent innovation: sold-out screenings in movie theaters of "live" opera performances by New York's Metropolitan Opera (the "Met") and other companies.

Perhaps the most evocatively American "classical" music is that of George Gershwin and Aaron Copland. Influenced by African-American rhythms and stories, Gershwin (1898–1937) is best known for *Rhapsody in Blue* and the opera *Porgy and Bess*. Copland (1900–90) captured the American landscape and spirit in his symphonies, opera, and film and ballet scores. Other important American composers are Samuel Barber and Leonard Bernstein, an extraordinary talent equally at home in Symphony Hall and, with the classic *West Side Story*, in the Broadway Theater.

The regular sponsors of classical series have been notoriously wary of modern music—New York's summer festival at Lincoln Center attracts subscribers by assuring them it's "Mostly Mozart"—but "minimalist" works by American contemporary composers Philip Glass, Steve Reich, and John Adams are increasingly reaching a wider audience.

What does patriotism sound like? A John Philip Sousa march. A marching band display or fireworks spectacular isn't complete without the "Stars and Stripes Forever." And the quintessential American experience? Sitting in a park listening to a free concert by the Boston Pops—a classical orchestra that plays popular all-American standards (with the obligatory backdrop of fireworks, of course).

Music

Perhaps the best way to experience America's music is on a cross-country drive. Skip the streaming audio and tune in instead to local FM stations where you'll hear New York rap, Kentucky bluegrass guitar, Miami's Latin rhythms, Nashville country, Louisiana zydeco, and the sunny California surf sound. Live music can be enjoyed at stops along the way—new bands in college towns, swaying gospel-singing church choirs, and rock giants at major stadiums.

Early African-American blues and gospel from America's cotton fields and churches evolved into jazz and rhythm and blues (R&B). Jazz—often regarded as the first truly American art form—found its voice in the street squares and funeral processions of New Orleans and has undergone many incarnations, including ragtime, swing,

Rock'n'Roll star Elvis Presley aka The King, 1968.

Motown legend and the Prince of Soul, Marvin Gaye, 1973.

big band, and bebop. The R&B sounds of James Brown and Chuck Berry were popularized by Elvis Presley. Black artists and producers spearheaded the evolution of contemporary music through soul singers of Detroit's Motown label in the 1960s, the disco sound of the 1970s, rap's arrival in the 1980s, and its transformation into hip-hop, dominating the world's musical airwaves to this day.

Just like with fast food, there's no need to tell you about pop, rock, or hip-hop. Contemporary music is America's most successful cultural export, so if it's popular here, there's a good chance you'll have heard it too.

Not so much in reverse, however. Many leading recording artists from other countries have failed to break into American markets, probably because of language differences—Americans want their pop (and their movies) in English, and even homegrown Tejano music and other Spanish-language genres rarely reach wider audiences. A rare exception has been the trendsetting K-Pop genre, whose Korean lyrics only occasionally make room for a word or two of English.

Books

America's literature explores the depth and breadth of the country's experience. It spans the horror and mystery stories of Edgar Allan Poe and the idealism of the transcendentalist writers Emerson and Thoreau, to the adrenaline-fueled works of the "Lost Generation" writer Ernest Hemingway and searing portrayals of the African-American experience. Great authors such as Fitzgerald, Faulkner, and Steinbeck used their talents to capture a nation that was making the twentieth century its own. Chandler and Hammett took us along the mean streets of big city crime. John Updike and John Cheever showed us the undercurrents of middle-class life in America's suburbs and small towns. And the prolific Stephen King continues to terrify us.

Half of the books sold in the USA are now purchased from Amazon, but bookstore chains and local independent stores hang on. Some independent retailers continued to offer book pick-up services during the coronavirus lockdowns,

John Steinbeck, 1939.

any many were able to bounce back when restrictions ended and book-hungry readers were able to browse the shelves once more.

A popular pastime for literate Americans is the book club, where small groups of readers meet periodically to praise or skewer the latest novel over nibbles and Chardonnay.

Visual Arts

Most major cities have at least one fine arts museum, often founded on the private collections that multi-millionaires of earlier generations picked up on their vacations to Europe. But although homegrown American art was a late starter, the country has caught up, producing outstanding artists, from Whistler to Warhol. Many great American artists may be unfamiliar names to the overseas visitor, because their works were snapped up by the nation's

The ancient Egyptian Temple of Dendur at the Metropolitan Museum of Art, New York City.

galleries and collections before the paint was dry.

A perfect way to meet new people? Dump those heavy outer layers in the coatroom and enjoy a winter afternoon exploring New York's "Met" (this time it's the Metropolitan Museum of Art, not the opera), maybe striking up a conversation over Van Gogh's *Irises* or a jazzy Jackson Pollock. (This also works for Washington, Chicago, Boston, Philadelphia, etc., but with different masterpieces.)

The USA remains a pioneer in the visual arts. As well as paintings, sculpture, and drawings, look out for museums and exhibitions devoted to photography, graphic design, and folk art.

Film

America didn't invent the movies, but it has more than made up for that omission. A perfect melding of art, science, and big business, America and cinema is a match made in Hollywood heaven. From Disney to Spielberg, from Pickford to Streep, from *Gone With the Wind* to *Titanic*, the list of American greats is virtually endless. American films have shaped our sensibilities over the century, usurping for many the role of literature in the process. A modern-day expression of populism, film also gives great insight into the American psyche.

Some lament that the Hollywood blockbuster has been "dumbed down," unfairly skewing the world's perception of American life. But while the multiplex in the local mall may be dominated by films based on comic book heroes, most towns have an arts cinema, catering to the strong following for independent and foreign films. In addition, many low-budget gems are now reaching audiences through the television screen. Read on.

Television

Ninety-nine percent of American households have at least one TV set, and broadcast television is still the number one medium. For decades, the "boob tube" depended on the airwaves, with national networks ABC, CBS, NBC and later Fox, plus every city's local station, Spanish-language channels like Univisión, and ad-free public broadcasting. Then came cable and satellite TV, squirting dozens of specialist channels—hundreds in some cities—into the home: 24-hour news such as CNN, MSNBC, and Fox News, as well as themed channels like MTV, Nickelodeon, ESPN, Animal Planet, Comedy Central, and many more. Dozens of radio channels were often included. For an extra fee, you could watch recent movies and exclusive programming on HBO (Home Box Office), Showtime, and other pay channels—"on demand," not tied to schedules.

Now there's the Internet, and home viewers are increasingly ditching the antennas, cutting the cable cord, and connecting their huge 4K Ultra HD flatscreen TVs (and their laptops and smartphones) to their home WiFi. Streaming services such as Netflix, Apple TV+, Hulu, and Amazon supply high-quality programming you can choose at your leisure—including the latest movies, whose instant availability is no longer a sign of low expectations (or poor box office takings). Most new TVs arrive with these premium services and apps built in.

Of course, although today's television offers a massive spectrum of stunningly high-quality, original programming from all sources—and any sport looks great in high definition—much of the programming is still highly repetitive. Those all-day, all-news channels, many openly flaunting a political bias, stretch every item to fill out the time, with a low fact-to-opinion ratio. The nightly local news still favors the visual over the verbal: "if it bleeds, it leads." For discerning viewers, there's the Public Broadcast System. Funded by viewer donations and corporate sponsorship— and nothing to do with the US government—it offers news analysis, educational programming, and British imports.

The TV equivalent of the Oscars are the annual Emmy awards. For those looking for something to watch, the most recent Emmy nominations are a good place to start.

Radio and Streaming

Just like TV, there's been a revolution in the way Americans get their sound. A 2021 CBS poll found that 41 percent use a streaming service (61 percent if you isolate the 18-34 age band), while only 31 percent tune into traditional broadcast radio stations. It helps that the only satellite radio in the nation—SiriusXM—is installed in more than half of all cars, delivering crystal-clear sound and an enormous range of programming options. Online platforms like Spotify and Apple Music compete for that digital audience. So what if you're likely to pay for the service—it beats hearing all those ads.

The Internet also supplies podcasts on all topics, typically updated daily or weekly. Americans make up half of the world's podcast listeners, and Apple alone gives its subscribers half a million to choose from. Comedy is the nation's current favorite, followed by news. And the classic AM/FM stations—more than 15,000 across the nation—still have their devoted fans. Just flick through the frequencies and you're bound to find a fitting soundtrack to your journey—rock, pop, urban, country, gospel or just those "oldies but goodies" that go back to your childhood (or your parents' childhood). If you prefer Beethoven to Bruno Mars, you may be lucky enough to find one of the few remaining classical stations. And, like all those podcasts, there's talk, talk, talk—news, politics, religion, sport, all filling the hours by inviting listeners to call in.

Want to escape the endless commercials? Just as there's publicly funded TV, there are public radio channels, a reliable source of thought-provoking, in-depth programs, while many college-based stations also play music ad-free.

Gaming

Video and online gaming is colossal in the USA. Americans spent an estimated $37 billion on gaming in 2021 alone— more than they spent on movies and music combined— and that's only expected to increase. More than two-thirds of Americans spend time playing computer-based games, and that rockets to nearly 100 percent when you focus on younger age groups. The average gamer is thirty-three years old, he's been playing for fourteen years, and he spends over fourteen hours a week clicking and tapping away. And that "he" is almost as likely to be a she.

A heads-up: in the USA "gaming" is also an alternative name for "gambling," so try not to confuse the two.

CHAPTER SEVEN

TRAVEL, HEALTH, & SAFETY

*"Go West, young man, go West and grow up
with the country"*

Horace Greeley, 1811–72

The tale of post-colonial America is a story of travel and exploration: the early discoveries of Lewis and Clarke's expedition to the Pacific, aided by the fifteen-year-old Indian woman Sacagawea, immortalized on an edition of the golden dollar coin; the covered wagons or "prairie schooners" that took families to new homes in the West; the great cattle drives of the 1860s and '70s, which spawned the legends of the cowboys; the first transcontinental railway, completed in 1869, that brought the six-month "sea to shining sea" overland trek down to just one week; and the classic twentieth-century adventure of Route 66, the "Main Street of America," best seen from the leather seats of a Corvette convertible with a Nelson Riddle big band arrangement on the AM radio.

Apart from the truly native Americans, the nation is descended from voyagers, whether they braved the savage

Atlantic in flimsy wooden ships or first stepped onto this brave new world from an Airbus at New York's JFK airport.

As we've noted, only a third of American citizens possess up-to-date passports (though before the Covid-19 shutdown, the number of people taking vacations abroad was steadily growing). When faced with such a tempting array of destinations at home—from the imposing skylines of its major cities to the jaw-dropping beauty of its national parks—you begin to understand why so many Americans are content sticking to their own territory: there are enough long journeys within the borders of this vast country to fill a lifetime of annual vacations.

The USA has a spectacular variety of landscapes and offers every conceivable activity. Interested in history? Pick up a musket and participate in a Civil War reconstruction in historic Virginia. Need an adrenaline surge? Try backcountry skiing in Utah or white-water rafting on the swift Colorado. Want to escape? Lose yourself in the fantasy land of Disney World or Las Vegas. There's enough variety to last a lifetime and the visitor really is spoiled for choice!

This book isn't designed to be an exhaustive travel guide; there's a plethora of wonderful travel books targeting different budgets and interests, and endless information online. However, for those who truly want to discover the people and places beyond the usual tourist traps, here are two pieces of advice. First, consider exploring one or two regions in depth, as opposed to darting from city to city. Second, eschew the motel and fast-food chains in favor of B&Bs and restaurants that offer local color and authenticity as opposed to corporate homogeneity.

ARRIVAL

The information here assumes that there are no current Covid-19 related travel restrictions in place, so make sure you check the latest procedures before you set out.

The United States Department of Homeland Security rigorously scrutinizes all travel documents. Visitors are usually required to show a passport, US visitor's visa, and a return plane ticket. A visa-waiver program (VWP) applies to many European and other countries, but users must carry an e-passport with a digital photograph. Other programs designed to speed up your processing, such as Global Entry and NEXUS, may apply depending on your nationality—check the Homeland Security website. Longer-stay travelers, such as students, will need a different type of entry visa and proof of finances. It's essential that you have the right information in your passport and other relevant paperwork, or you may be on your way home again without leaving the airport. If in doubt, check with the US embassy or consulate that's closest to your hometown, preferably several weeks before your trip, especially if you want to use a program that may require an interview.

You'll need to complete immigration and customs forms, which you'll probably receive on the airplane or ship just before you land.

On arrival—and for most visitors, that's an airport—the first stop will be Immigration, where you'll probably be asked the purpose of your visit, how long you're staying, and possibly where you're planning to travel. (A hint: know the answers to these questions.) Some airports may start the process by collecting some information at online kiosks. Then you collect your baggage and filter through Customs. (Another hint: don't take any chances. Check with the Customs and Border Patrol Web site [www.cbp.gov] ahead of time to make sure you're not carrying something that could get you into trouble.)

And then . . . you're in America. If you've already reserved a rental car, head for the desk or the courtesy phone for the rental company. That's also the first stop if you want a car without a reservation (have a driver's license and credit card handy). For buses, trains, and taxis to your hotel or the business district, head out of the terminal—which may be a short walk or a considerable hike, depending on the airport—and look for the signs. Information desks and uniformed personnel will help. You may also get several whispered offers of trips in unlicensed cabs or private limos. It's best to ignore them and pick up a licensed taxi from the proper "stand," even if the wait is longer. Most official taxis are metered, but this can vary from city to city.

HITTING THE ROAD

From its stately cities to its sprawling suburbs, America was designed for the citizen with personal transportation. And when the horse and buggy gave way to the automobile, twentieth-century urban planners responded with communities that made full use of the nation's wide-open spaces. While much of the world strolls to the village store or market every morning, the suburban American family

An aerial view of downtown New York.

motors once a week to the nearest strip mall, maybe several miles from home, to fill up the minivan at some vast supermarket, surrounded by a sea of parking spaces. Unless you live in one of the larger cities—such as New York, which offsets its glacial traffic movement and exorbitant parking costs with effective public transportation—a car is a necessity in America. No surprise then that the USA, with less than 5 percent of the world's population, burns 14 percent of the world's oil production on road transportation alone. Government investment in electric vehicle infrastructure should help to reduce this figure in future.

Those who can't resist the romance of a road trip will find American drivers to be neither the most courteous nor the most aggressive (despite highly publicized reports of "road rage"). Americans will also tell you that they don't have to look at the license plate of the car in front to tell which state the driver is from. Apparently, there are great regional variations in styles of driving! (We're looking at you, Boston.)

Car Rentals

Car rental outlets exist everywhere, although rates will be more affordable outside the major cities and airports. Options range from opulent sedans or sporty convertibles to "rent-a-wrecks" for those with little pride and a budget to match. Electric vehicles (EVs) are now commonly available, and though some drivers may suffer "range anxiety," improved batteries and charging infrastructure, particularly inside cities, mean they are a good option for most. Remember to factor in the size of car, taxes, mandatory insurance, and fuel mileage when comparison shopping to obtain the most favorable rates.

Driving Permits

While most car rental agencies will accept your national driver's license, an international license can be a valuable English-language photo ID document to carry with you. It must be issued in the same country as your driver's license.

Navigation Needs

If you're planning a long car trip during your visit—a necessity for some locations, but a great way to see the country—then make sure you can access a GPS-based mapping service such as MapQuest or Google Maps, either built into the car or through your smartphone. ("Waze" is a popular alternative, because of its crowd-sourced information about traffic and police patrols—not that you were planning on speeding.) You may still find a printed driver's atlas in a convenience store at a highway rest stop.

Some Basic Rules of the Road

Be aware that driving laws vary slightly from state to state. Nevertheless, nationwide, you should wear seat belts and never drive under the influence of alcohol or drugs.

Drive on the right. When making a left turn, cross in front of any car facing you that's stopped to make its own left turn unless a sign tells you otherwise. You can turn right at a red light (after you've stopped and if no traffic's coming from the left), except if there's a sign to wait for the green light. But be aware that you can't turn on a red light in any borough of New York City.

Speed limits are strictly enforced by radar-toting highway patrol or sheriff's officers. Fines can be stiff. Speed limits range from 55 mph (89 kmph) on urban roads to 75 mph (121 kmph) on rural highways. In urban areas, speed limits change frequently, particularly in the vicinity of a school, so watch for signs. Special signs listing local restrictions and speed limits are often posted at city limits.

ROAD SENSE

There are three types of major road. The letter "I" indicates an Interstate Highway, "US" a US Highway, and "Rte" (route) a local or state highway.

The system of interstate road numbers is as follows. Even-numbered interstates (for example, I-80) run east–west (with the lowest numbers starting in the south). Odd-numbered routes (I-15) run north–south (the lowest numbers start in the west).

An expressway is a high-speed divided highway for through traffic with fully or partially controlled access. Expressways have entrance and exit ramps and may or may not have tolls. The term "expressway" is used interchangeably with "thruway," and "divided" means the two streams of traffic may or may not be separated by a cement or metal barrier or by landscaping.

A highway, meanwhile, typically goes through cities rather than bypassing them as expressways do, and may or may not be divided.

A turnpike is traditionally a toll-road—although you may also have to pay tolls on thruways, expressways, and "parkways," which are basically divided highways that restricts commercial traffic. Most tolls use an electric transponder system, such as "E-Z Pass," which reads your car tag as you drive through. If you have a rental car, make sure you ask how your agency handles tolls for visitors. You may still be able to use cash if you don't mind slowing down at a booth, although many toll stations have discontinued this option.

TAKING FLIGHT

Americans like to drive, and the highway system is well developed and generally well maintained, but for the trip that takes nearly a day or longer on the road, the second choice of travel methods is the airplane, preferred by a wide margin over the passenger train—

if you can find one. For the tourist with a long way to go, a fly-drive package might be the best option.

For the savvy traveler, when it comes to domestic flights, it's a buyer's market. The existence of no-frills airlines and regular price wars among carriers make for a wide range of fare options (sometimes even for the same seat). The best place to start is one of the many apps and Web sites that compare prices and availability, such as Trip Advisor and Expedia. If you can be flexible, either book well in advance or pick up a last-minute discount price. If you're willing to fly during an off-peak season and to take a circuitous route involving change(s) of plane, you can further reduce travel costs.

Once you've booked, make sure the airline can reach you in case of last-minute changes. You won't have to face Customs and Immigration on internal flights—although you may need your passport as your photo ID—but security checks can be as strict as for international travel, and may include full-body scans or pat-downs, X-rays of all hand baggage and even shoes, and restrictions on liquids in the cabin. Other limitations or rules may depend on current public health issues. Follow your airline's advice about the amount of time you need for pre-boarding. If you turn up at the airport five minutes before your flight, you've missed it!

To save time waiting for checked bags and cases—and to save the fees that some no-frills airlines charge—many Americans cram all they need for a trip into their hand baggage. Expect storage space in the main cabin to be limited.

Amtrak passengers enjoy views of Colorado's Rocky Mountains from their carriage.

RIDING THE RAILS

While the nationwide train system, Amtrak, is much maligned by Americans, train travel is still a relaxing way to cover a lot of ground.

Amtrak's intercity network is not as comprehensive as the long-distance bus routes and can be as expensive as air travel. However, it does reach over five hundred destinations and as most stations are in downtown areas, train travel can save the time and money spent getting to and from airports. The best-served cities are those on the northwest "corridor," with frequent, regular services from Boston through New York, Baltimore, Philadelphia to Washington, D.C. For a premium, you can travel between these cities on the high-speed Acela trains, which can get up to 150 mph on some stretches of the track.

Amtrak has more than thirty other major routes around the country, serving the major cities of most states and crossing into Canada on some routes. The Amtrak Web site (www.amtrak.com) will tell you where the trains run and how long each trip can take.

GET ON THE BUS

Movies often depict long-distance bus travel in the United States as a service for society's disenfranchised and misfits. The bus stations may seem a little seedy, but the truth is that bus travel offers a reliable service for the seasoned, low-budget traveler willing to sit for twenty-eight hours to get from New York to Miami. Buses cover more ground in the USA than airlines, they have similar in-transit amenities (although you bring your own food and drink), and you certainly get to meet Americans.

LOCAL PUBLIC TRANSPORTATION

Perhaps because the USA is a car-dependent nation, public transport (or "mass transit") is generally not as comprehensive or efficient as in other countries. Exceptions are the subway systems of New York, Washington D.C., Chicago, and San Francisco, which service most tourist destinations, but are best avoided at rush hour!

The standard of local bus services in towns and cities is highly variable, and so is how you pay. Some companies allow you to purchase your ticket at a machine at the bus stand or use a general pre-purchased farecard. Others allow you to pay for your trip online or, increasingly, download the relevant company app to purchase your ticket, which is scanned when you board. You may even find a driver who still takes cash! We suggest you check online ahead of time.

Taxis

Taxis generally run on a metered system and can be hailed on streets in some cities if the "for hire" sign is illuminated. For those in a hurry, most cities are serviced by one or more of the popular ride-hailing apps, such as Uber, Lyft, and Curb. One of the most publicized traits of cab drivers in large cities is their ethnic diversity, with a survey revealing that nine out of ten new drivers in New York are immigrants, hailing from eighty-four different countries. While this makes for interesting conversation, you shouldn't assume that all drivers automatically know the way to your destination. Today, most will use a navigation system of some sort. Cabs picked up on the street increasingly use credit card readers to collect fares, and as we've noted, tipping is expected.

WHERE TO STAY

The weary traveler has a huge range of accommodation options catering to different budgets and preferences. The choices range from no-frills youth hostels to luxury resorts and New Age spas, and everything in between.

Even campsites give an insight into the broad spectrum of American vacation habits, with dwellings ranging from humble canvas tents to motor homes on wheels for those who like to take all modern conveniences—including the kitchen sink—on vacation. You can avoid soulless highway motels by hitting the back roads and enjoying the personal touch of moderately priced B&Bs and country inns. Apps such as Airbnb allow a look into how the locals live, while your favorite booking sites are primed with reviews and often discounts, too.

Where's the Restroom?

Visitors are often surprised and dismayed at the scarcity of public lavatories in the USA. Railway, bus, and service stations usually have them, but better facilities are to be found in department stores, museums, and restaurants. Rest stops on the highways are usually well maintained, despite (or perhaps because of) the high volume of traffic.

"Where Is It?"

In America, use "bathroom" in a private house, "restroom" in a public facility, and "men's room" or "ladies' room" in a restaurant, theater, or hotel.

HEALTH

The United States is relatively free of health risks (assuming your coronavirus protection is up to date, of course), but visitors should still consider taking out the maximum possible health insurance. The multitiered US healthcare system is complex and astoundingly expensive. Unless it is truly an emergency, a visit to the ER (emergency room) should be avoided. Although an ER is legally required to treat you, you may expect a long wait and a very large bill—even something simple like strep throat could cost well over $1,000.

Look out instead for "Urgent Care" or "Walk-in Care" centers that may be available—although not a 24-hour service—and that are intended for nonemergency care.

Hospitals will request a credit card or proof of insurance coverage before any diagnosis or treatment. If you do need to receive medical attention, rest assured that standards are extremely high. Any lingering pain once you return home is likely to be from hefty doctors' or hospital bills.

Before You Leave Home

You can't predict every eventuality, so it's essential to take out comprehensive travel insurance for your trip. Coverage should include medical treatment, emergency repatriation, travel delays or cancellations, ticket loss, property theft or loss, and personal liability. Check to see if your credit card already covers car rental and/or travel insurance.

SAFETY AND SECURITY

As a travel destination, America is one of the safest places in the world. Despite lingering impressions of the Wild West and the gangster days of Prohibition, most towns offer little risk of crime, the people are friendly and approachable, and the police are happy to help a puzzled tourist. Of course, you should take reasonable precautions, especially in cities.

In terms of personal safety, general commonsense rules apply. Beware of pickpockets in crowded areas. Avoid dark, deserted streets and empty train or subway cars. Use ATMs in daylight, preferably inside a bank. Keep your wallet in your front pocket. Leave passports and valuables in hotel safe deposit boxes. Be sure to take photocopies of your passport, visa, and plane tickets and keep them separate from your travel documents.

When renting a car, ask the agent to explain the safest route to your desired destination so as to avoid having to navigate a downtown area at night. Hitchhiking isn't recommended and may well be illegal, depending on state and even city laws. Most importantly, try to blend in and avoid looking like a camera-wielding, map-toting tourist, which is thankfully more easily done today now that everything you need is on the smartphone in your back pocket.

The "9/11" terrorist attacks in 2001 resulted in a heightened awareness of the need for security. As such, in addition to the extra time you now need to leave before airline flights, you'll probably find there are security checks at many public venues and office buildings.

EMERGENCIES

For police, fire, or ambulance services, call 911 toll free.

Don't Shoot, It's Only Me!

In the wake of so many horrific stories of gun violence emanating from the United States, outsiders might question why gun ownership is not outlawed altogether. The "right to bear arms" (the Second Amendment) was enshrined in the Constitution in the post-Revolutionary era to equip local militias to defend their hard-won land. Today the British pose less of a threat—and in most of the 44 percent of American households that have a gun, the firearms are legally registered as being for personal protection or recreational use. One in five households acquired a gun since the outbreak of Covid-19 in 2020

Gun ownership continues to be a matter that polarizes American public opinion, however. Support for the gun lobby tends to be regionally based, with a heavy concentration in the hunting, shooting, and fishing states. A bipartisan bill in 2022 that included tougher background checks on purchases was the first gun control measure to pass in three decades, but many citizens felt it was too tentative.

BATTEN DOWN THE HATCHES

Given the continent's extreme weather patterns, rarely a year goes by without one headline-making natural disaster. These include hurricanes pounding the Gulf or the eastern seaboard, snowstorms paralyzing cities on the eastern seaboard, tornadoes tearing through "tornado alley" in the Midwest, and increasingly, western forest fires, fueled by late summer winds and drought conditions aggravated by global warming. Hurricane Ian in 2022 was the deadliest hurricane to hit Florida for over eighty years. Fortunately, the US meteorological services are able to predict conditions likely to produce extreme weather accurately, and residents in affected areas are usually well prepared to react to such occurrences. Nevertheless, seasonal weather patterns should be taken into account when planning your trip.

No Lions, No Tigers, But Some Bears

America has its share of inconvenient wildlife, from roaming alligators in Florida to testy rattlesnakes in the Southwest to disease-carrying but microscopic deer ticks in New England. (The most irritating? Probably the mosquito. Use a repellant if you hear a buzzing on sultry summer evenings.) And whatever you do, don't annoy a skunk!

However, in most locations, you're unlikely to encounter any dangerous wildlife, unless you're heading off into the "back country," in which case take the advice of an expert, such as one of the experienced and well-trained park rangers who work for the National Park Service. The National Park System covers 84 million acres/340,000 sq. km of America's most beautiful and enticing landscapes and monuments.

In hot areas, remember to carry plenty of water and use sunscreen. In cold areas—and nightfall can bring some precipitous drops in temperature, even in the desert lands—carry extra layers of clothing. And in all locations, make sure your cell phone is fully charged before you leave.

CHAPTER EIGHT

BUSINESS BRIEFING

"Yankees and Dollars have such inextricable association that the words ought to rhyme."

Ralph Waldo Emerson, Journal Entry, 1840

The United States is by far the wealthiest country in the world with a GDP that's one-third greater than China's, its nearest rival (at current trends, however, the USA is scheduled to slip to second place by the year 2030). America has a highly diversified industrial and service-based economy. Its devotion to capitalism and the free market is absolute and unshakable, despite the economic ups and downs of the twenty-first century so far.

Before the pandemic struck, America was on a historic high. Action taken, first by President Bush and then picked up by President Obama, had dragged the nation out of a slew of crises, starting with the subprime mortgage crisis that led to 2009's "Great Recession," characterized as the worst economic meltdown since the Great Depression. In a striking one-eighty, the 2010s was the first decade without a US recession since record-keeping began in the 1850s. The

S&P 500 Index rose in nine of the ten years, unemployment plunged to a fifty-year low, inflation tanked, and Obama's Affordable Care Act led to a substantial decline in the number of Americans without health insurance. (The federal deficit—indicating government spending—was relentlessly creeping up, but interest rates were so low, politicians left it on the back-burner.)

And then came Covid-19, infecting the last year of Trump's presidency and pulling the legs out from underneath that still-rosy economy (see page 53). America screeched to a halt as lockdowns were rapidly imposed. Entire industries shut down—the Big Three car manufacturers (GM, Ford, Chrysler) stopped production completely. Stores and restaurants closed, and freshly unemployed parents found themselves spending twenty-four hours a day with their children, whose schools had been shuttered. There were a record 3.3 million new claims for unemployment benefits in a single week in March 2020—the previous record had been 700,000, forty years earlier. Altogether, 25 million people were unemployed for at least part of the pandemic.

Unsurprisingly, the US stock market plummeted in early 2020, as did markets across the world, but it started to recover almost immediately and had regained its pre-crash level before the end of the year.

Covid-19 is now largely tamed, America has returned to work—if sometimes reluctantly after the cosy convenience of that home office—and everyday life has resumed. The economic outlook remains uncertain, however, as the US faces its share of global inflation and supply-chain issues exacerbated by the Russian invasion of Ukraine and bubbling political tensions in the Far East.

Meanwhile, on the labor front generally, the strength and political influence of the trade union movement has diminished since its heyday in the 1930s, as former union strongholds, such as manufacturing, decline. Indeed, it's estimated that 60 percent of new jobs in the information-age economy require skills currently held by just 20 percent of the workforce. The growing skills and resultant wealth gap is likely to remain a long-term challenge for America's twenty-first-century politicians and employers.

As the lure of cheap labor continues to drive production overseas, the "Made in the USA" label is becoming ever scarcer. Telephone and online technical support is more likely to be based in New Delhi than New York. Global consumers are ambivalent—they love American fast food but fear what has been dubbed "coca-colonization."

English remains the lingua franca of business, and American management philosophies are still internationally embraced. Yet US companies are learning that they can increase effectiveness—and be better global citizens—if they demonstrate cultural understanding and sensitivity overseas.

SNAPSHOT OF THE AMERICAN WORKPLACE

The American working environment is in a period of ongoing change that began even before Covid-19 arrived and reshaped people's working lives. Rising costs have seen employers increasingly offer part-time or shared jobs, or outsourcing to external contractors. Change is constant as companies are restructured, work teams become "virtual," and flexible work arrangements become the norm. Turnover is high because regular job-hopping is considered a résumé builder. The cradle-to-grave job mentality is long gone, and employees today are expected to take charge of their own career management. Employers expect ethical behavior and results; employees give it their all—until a better job offer comes along.

Policies, procedures, and practices govern every aspect of company life. In addition to enforcing equal opportunity legislation, corporate America has introduced diversity initiatives, promoting the employment and advancement of women and minorities. Sensitivity training is given to prevent discrimination and sexual harassment.

Roles are flexible, hierarchy is fluid, and functions are specialized. In today's "flatter" organization there's no stigma attached to a lateral move to develop new skills, or even to reporting to a former "fast track" protégé. The organization is "boundaryless," which means people are comfortable communicating up and down the pyramid, or across functional departments.

The length of the working day depends on the company, industry, and seniority of the employee. Administrative staff may do a straight nine to five, or put in "face time"— wanting to be seen at their desks. As we've seen, many workers, particularly professional people, may work excessively long hours, even sacrificing weekends and vacation days—willingly or otherwise. Foreign visitors often notice a paradox—on the surface, workers are informal and socialize freely, yet the volume and pace of work seem intense, and the employee who doesn't, when asked, admit to being "busy" may risk becoming the ex-employee. Federal Express envelopes are preprinted with the phrase "Extremely Urgent." During the pandemic, many workers found they could function well from their homes. Initially, managers were in favor of a full return to the office, seeing a value in human contact—and direct supervision. However, many companies have since embarked on a blended approach.

A typical office has an open-plan layout with partitioned cubicles, although the boss still gets the corner office with the best view, four walls, and a door. Managers are expected to be accessible and keep an "open-door" policy. Schedules and privacy should be respected. All but the most senior executives answer their own phone and are expected to keep on top of their online messages.

The office may briefly stop for a birthday, wedding, or baby "shower" celebration during work hours, with coworkers all contributing to a communal gift. Commutes are long, so there's little after-hours socializing. Companies usually arrange regular social events, however, such as a family picnic or softball game, or occasional Friday evening drinks.

The 24/7 Lifestyle

The spirit of constant urgency that has long haunted American business got a boost with the growth of electronic communications, especially that crucial moment when the telephone switched its attachment from a location to a person and became "smart." Now, nobody can use the "out of the office" excuse to dodge contact, and if the person you need isn't responding, you can send a text or fire off an email.

Many people actually prefer this alternative to face-to-face communication. Text-based programs and email are used extensively. Voicemail is vanishing, and people don't always check recorded messages during the working day. Colleagues in adjoining cubicles will sometimes text or WhatsApp each other—it's fast, it's efficient, and an electronic "paper trail" is left, and you can cover your professional posterior by copying messages to anyone who's remotely connected to the project. For many managers, messaging has transformed the nature of work, although much time is still spent reviewing the email inbox and deleting the irrelevant "FYI" copies. "I'm down to three hundred unread messages," boasted a human resources manager to one of the authors, after several weekend hours with the laptop.

The constant checking of smartphones—at all hours—has become a feature of modern behavior. It doesn't mean it isn't rude when your dinner companion tunes out your conversation and checks his or her iPhone for the fifteenth time!

Dress Code
Dress codes vary depending on the industry and corporate culture. At the more formal end of the sartorial spectrum, men typically wear dark suits, and women

dresses or skirts or pant suits. Many companies have instituted "casual Fridays," and it's not unusual for a business to have a relaxed dress code for the office but insist on changing into formal clothes for a client meeting. While this dress code allows for greater comfort, some grumble that it requires them to buy a second "uniform," usually chinos (khaki pants) with an open-necked "dress shirt" (long-sleeved, buttoned shirt) for men, and casual skirt or pants and top for women.

Professional clothes in general are expected to be of good quality but not overly stylish. Women's makeup and jewelry should be understated. If in doubt, always err on the side of conservatism. A confident posture, personal hygiene, and good grooming are all essential.

If you are in any doubt about what to wear for an initial business meeting, go with the more formal option.

First Impressions

Remember, "you never get a second chance to make a first impression." You'll be judged on your conduct and appearance. Sloppy manners or inappropriate behavior may sink a deal or relationship.

At initial meetings, Americans often seek common ground, common experiences, to form a quick rapport—in business, that might be a shared former employer, shared acquaintances, or a college fraternity or sorority. It's a moment of social bonding that isn't intended to be the start of a beautiful friendship, just a step toward a better working relationship.

Carry a Card?

Fewer people carry paper business cards these days, preferring the digital exchange afforded by a smartphone and a LinkedIn profile. If a card is presented, it won't be respectfully scrutinized, Asia style, and indeed may be tucked directly into a wallet.

Promote Yourself!

People from more modest cultures often find the American manner brash and boastful. An American would reply that you don't get ahead by waiting for other people to notice your talents, especially in a competitive business world, and he or she in turn has little patience with the kind of "amateurism" that values a valiant effort in the absence of tangible results. This "achievement orientation" may appear arrogant to outsiders, but is a cherished ideal and a powerful inner motivator that propels Americans forward in their pursuit of excellence.

And this immodesty is not just for the "psychic income" of fame and respect. There's real money involved. Most larger corporations operate as a meritocracy, giving salary increases, promotions, and above all a bigger share of the bonus pool to the individuals who contribute the most to company profits. The ambitious executive is literally invested in his or her own success.

An American will tell you that they're taught to believe in themselves, to put their best foot forward, and to stand out from the crowd. In such a big country, survival of the fittest rules. As one mid-level manager put it, "To compete, I need to be both my own best product and sales promoter." Professional people even hone their "elevator pitch," encapsulating in thirty seconds who they are and what they do.

Competition can be seen in every walk of life, from beauty pageants to "employee of the month" to July 4 hot-dog-eating contests. The drive to be first, highest, quickest, or just plain best has inspired Americans to accomplish extraordinary feats—but you'll only know the names of those who came first as "winner takes all." In other nations, an Olympic silver medal is a cause for jubilation; for an American athlete, it's a sign that you failed to win gold. In this culture, as famed football coach Vince Lombardi once said, "Second place is the first loser."

THE BOTTOM LINE

Americans don't feel as great a need to know the people they do business with as other cultures. Trust is placed in lawyers and contracts, not in people. Rules are made and applied universally to all. Deals are swayed by a client's reputation, by profit margins, or delivery time—not simply by the nature of the relationship.

In this "high task," "low relationship" society everything is systematized. While Latin American employees may rely on the long-term patronage of a patriarchal boss, newly appointed Americans are assigned a temporary "mentor" to help them navigate the new organization. Meanwhile, the savvy professional will develop a "network"—a loose-knit group of professional acquaintances who support each other on a reciprocal basis. Job-hunting is still a matter of who you know: 85 percent of jobs are secured through networking contacts—LinkedIn has over 800 million members worldwide—and 70 percent of job openings are never formally advertised.

MANAGEMENT STYLE

A good manager is expected to set goals, be action-oriented, and deliver results. The command-and-control style manager doesn't cut it here. To describe the preferred US management style, the analogy of the sports coach is often used. The manager will provide strategy and resources, and then cheerlead from the sidelines as the player "runs with the ball." The approach is to empower a subordinate to show initiative, make decisions, and be an independent contributor. "Don't bring me a problem—bring me the solution" is the mantra. The plethora of management books suggests that while great leaders may be born, a good manager can be developed.

Managers are evaluated on developing others, as well as on their own performance. The annual appraisal is an inclusive process, with employees being evaluated against mutually agreed-upon goals or objectives, and confidential feedback sought from peers and subordinates.

IF YOU'RE STANDING STILL, YOU'RE MOVING BACKWARD

While older societies might rely on precedent for wisdom and direction, the Americans look to the future for their inspiration. They are masters of reinvention, of generating and managing change. They may seem impetuous to outsiders. Americans have a "just do it" approach to business. They prefer "learning by doing" to cautious planning. Business is a moving target, so problem-solving and decision-making will provide short-term solutions, and not be etched in stone.

WORKING AS A UNIT

The American workplace is increasingly a team-oriented environment. The definition of "team" here is a group of individuals who work together to achieve a common objective. As we noted when considering individualism, it isn't the harmonious, consensus-driven model of Asia. Members are selected for their different areas of expertise, and may receive "team building skills" training to be a cohesive and effective unit.

Unfortunately, many companies send mixed messages. As we've seen, corporations are meritocracies, and as their workers scale the pyramid of power, the competition for the next promotion becomes tighter. When employees become personally invested in their own career—a level of devotion to the company that's positively encouraged—

there's a limit to the amount of teamwork they'll offer to coworkers who are also rivals for the next-level job, or whose success on the team project might cut into their own share of the incentive compensation.

> ### The Team
> Promoters of teamwork declare there's no "I" in team. Individualists wryly point out that the word does contain the letters "M" and "E."

MEETINGS

Meetings can serve a variety of purposes, from an impromptu ten-minute team catch-up to a preplanned, lengthier affair, with a detailed agenda and recorded minutes. At the close, roles and tasks are assigned and an action plan with deadlines is established.

As with many aspects of American life, a meeting is a democratic process. If it's in person and not on an online platform like Zoom or Microsoft Teams, the seating plan will be informal, and an assigned facilitator rather than the most senior person may lead the proceedings—although it's still not a good idea to interrupt the boss, no matter how long he or she takes to make a point. Individuals from all hierarchical levels are encouraged to contribute, and competing viewpoints are openly expressed, adding "creative tension" to the process. For the most part, individuals diplomatically acknowledge each other's point of view and "piggyback" (build) on each other's ideas.

Newcomers are often shocked to note how everyone competes for the floor, sometimes with seemingly redundant statements. Stemming from the educational system, individuals are evaluated on the level of their participation as well as the quality of contributions. Social Darwinism prevails even in meetings, and you need to take every opportunity to make your mark, so speak up. Although brainstorming meetings may be a little too unstructured or wacky for some people, Americans find them an effective way to generate creative ideas or solutions.

For a successful meeting, be punctual (signal if you're running late), be well presented, and be meticulously prepared.

PRESENTATIONS

Style or substance? When making a presentation, Americans will expect you to have both. Some cultures are more literal in approach, others prefer lengthy discussions to build trust. By contrast, Americans are visually oriented and prefer their presentations to be entertaining and high tech, whether it's for an in-person meeting or an online gathering. A brisk pace, persuasive tone, and anecdotal evidence are used to outline a proposal's merits. As Millennials have risen in the corporate world, attention spans have shrunk. Typical sessions will be brief (thirty to forty-five minutes) and well structured. Handouts, including hard data and "decks" (copies of a presentation), are usually made available. Time for feedback or a "Q&A" (question-and-answer session) will be allocated.

NEGOTIATIONS

The American negotiating style tends to be a "hard sell"—sometimes characterized as sledgehammer subtlety combined with missionary zeal! A strong pitch about a product's, or individual's, strengths may sound boastful to you, but it's meant to inspire confidence and trust. It's also consistent with the penchant for logical reasoning, directness, and comfort with self-promotion.

American negotiators may have little familiarity with, or patience for, the formal business protocol, indirect communication style, or consensual decision-making practices of other countries. Their focus is on the short term and the "big picture": securing the best deal in a timely manner. Their approach is informal, cordial, and straightforward. The US team will reveal its position and expect the other party to engage in a competitive bargaining process. If an impasse is reached, American tenacity, creativity, and persuasiveness will come to the fore. Despite the "hard sell" tactics, negotiating partners shouldn't feel pressured into making a decision. The Americans expect their counterparts across the table to be similarly pragmatic and single-minded in trying to secure a favorable deal. The greatest source of frustration for American negotiators is feeling that they're being "strung along," or that their negotiating partners don't have the authority to make the necessary decisions.

Note: Americans like to walk away from a meeting having secured a verbal agreement—the details will be hammered out later. Thus, a handshake (real or notional) may "seal the deal," but the agreement isn't in place until the ink on the contract is dry. But generally, they assume "yes" means "I agree." If you come from a culture where saying "yes" is a polite way of expressing understanding, but not a final agreement, you may run into some problems.

Silence is Not Golden

The Tokyo-based negotiations between an American company and a Japanese vendor, having started well, unraveled on the last day. The Americans were focused on "bottom line" details: price and delivery dates. The Japanese were more concerned about process—and trust. Whenever the Japanese paused to reflect carefully on their counterparts' position, the Americans jumped in to fill the pause. The Americans interpreted the Japanese silence around the table as intransigence; the Japanese construed the American discomfort with silence as an unwillingness to listen. Clearly each party had come to the table equipped with their negotiating strategy, but with little understanding of the other party's cultural style.

CEO of US multinational investment bank Citigroup, Jane Fraser.

WOMEN IN BUSINESS

Despite a temporary dip during the pandemic, women now make up more than half of the American workforce. They're increasingly represented at the management level and are making their mark in nontraditional fields. Overt discrimination, sexism, and inappropriate behavior toward women is dealt with swiftly in today's business culture, helped by the "Me Too" movement, which emboldens victims of harassment and sexual assault to seek justice. However, many contend that subtle discrimination still exists, preventing women from rising above the "glass ceiling." In terms of advancement opportunities, many working mothers feel they're diverted from the "fast track" to the "mommy track." Flexible hours, child care, and pay parity are improving, especially in more "enlightened" companies, but they remain hurdles.

BUSINESS ENTERTAINING

Foreign business visitors shouldn't expect VIP treatment. Even the most senior executive won't be picked up from an airport or hotel. Business entertaining is only likely to occur for a specific reason: to impress a potential client or for a "deal-closing" dinner. Don't let the informal dress and social chit-chat fool you. Americans take their business seriously. Behavior is relaxed but relatively restrained. The two-martini lunch became the two-Perrier lunch long ago. If in doubt about ordering an alcoholic drink, even at dinner, take your cues from your host. The meal will start with small talk but quickly get down to business. Cocktail parties are juggling acts—make sure you always have one hand free of food and drink to greet people.

Americans aren't accustomed to receiving and giving gifts in business settings and wouldn't expect it.

CHAPTER NINE

COMMUNICATING

LINGUISTIC TRADITIONS

From street slang to psychobabble, business jargon to catchphrases, the American language provides a window into the ever-changing culture. The Americans have always loved to share their thoughts and feelings. Benjamin Franklin's homespun proverbs and Mark Twain's witticisms have been handed down through the generations. In this millennium, philosophy is laced with humor and more likely to come from a fridge magnet, bumper sticker, or a viral tweet—and Americans keep their one-liners short: only one percent of all tweets bump up against the platform's 280-character limit.

Historically, language has been at the forefront in defining America's distinct cultural identity. Connecticut's Noah Webster published the first American-English dictionary in 1806, believing that a distinctive American language was a further mark of independence from the British. Webster's dictionary included new American vocabulary, such as skunk and chowder. Webster also modified needlessly complicated spellings, changing centre to center, plough to plow, and colour to color.

More recently, Americans have debated whether immigrant children should be provided with bilingual education. While the wheels of government turn slowly on such issues, corporate America acts. TV and radio stations targeting different language groups abound. The language of billboards reflects the demographics of the neighborhood. Call any helpline and you get a Spanish-speaking option, and many bank ATMs have added Chinese.

It's estimated that one in five people speak a mother tongue other than English. Spanish is the second-most spoken language in the USA, with 41 million people using it at home. Meanwhile, there are still enclaves that operate exclusively in the language of the old country— Yiddish is common in certain parts of Brooklyn, and the Amish communities of Pennsylvania and Ohio communicate in a dialect of German.

Here's a smattering of words borrowed from other languages that have been incorporated into the American lexicon: moose and caucus (Native American), chocolate (Aztec), tycoon (Mandarin), saloon and café (French), cookie (Dutch), glitch, schmooze, and chutzpah (Yiddish), kindergarten and delicatessen (German). The all-American hamburger? Also German.

Divided by a Common Language

George Bernard Shaw is reputed to have said that America and England were "two countries divided by a common language." There are differences in spelling, vocabulary, and idiom. To table a motion means to put something on the agenda in the UK; in the USA it means to remove it. The British stand for election while dynamic Americans run for office. Americans break the ice; Brits melt it. Revealingly, the British "take" a decision, while Americans "make" one.

COMMUNICATION STYLE

Have a great day! Terrific suit! Nice job! American exchanges generally tend to be informal, laced with superlatives, with an exclamation point on the end. Everything is given a positive twist, a "challenge" euphemistically being transformed into an "opportunity."

In most situations, Americans pride themselves on treating everyone in the same upbeat manner. They'll expect to be on first-name terms, regardless of age or rank. Occupational titles such as Doctor, Officer, or Professor may be used at work only. The title "Ms." covers both married and unmarried women, but is mainly used in written communication. Names are often shortened, with or without the owner's permission, and nicknames are common. Americans excel at remembering—and making frequent use of—the first names of the people they meet.

Generally with Americans, what you see (or hear) is what you get, particularly in business. There's no "beating around the bush." "Honesty is the best policy," so directness is preferred over politeness and diplomacy. This may sound blunt to the European ear, used to an eloquent discourse or intellectual debate. Americans, however, prefer exchanges to be brief, clear, and precise—preferably delivered in a sound bite. The Americans express their ideas and emotions more freely than, for example, northern Europeans, although profanity is still frowned upon in public. Table thumping and raised voices indicate poor self-control and may be judged accordingly. Personal disputes are considered socially disruptive and are handled with customary American pragmatism. (Until it's time to get lawyers involved, in which case, "see you in court.")

Quick off the Mark

Picture this: a German completes a business presentation to three clients. The Japanese sits back and respectfully considers what he's heard. The English woman mentally formulates a carefully constructed, articulate response. The American? Jumps right in. Timing and spontaneity are of the essence. It's important to show you can think on your feet, "tell it like it is," and act quickly. It all comes down to performance and results.

The style of thinking is a linear progression through a logical sequence of facts to one clear conclusion—cause and effect, connect the dots. Americans place trust in objective, concrete facts and data. Information is conveyed in the explicit verbal message. There's no need for subtle, nonverbal gestures, hidden meanings, or extraneous information. Just the facts, ma'am, will do. Written reports will be headed with a brief "executive summary"— probably in bullet points.

Sporting Talk

The competitive world of sports provides perfect analogies for American business speak. American managers dutifully espouse the latest buzz words—bandwidth, non-fungible, the "new normal"—but are more comfortable "stepping up to the plate" to "touch all the bases" and "hit a home run!" Approximate figures are described as "in the ballpark."

Small Talk

"So, how about those Mets?" "Hot enough for ya?" A casual conversation is often opened with a rhetorical question. Small talk is confined to safe topics—TV programs, sports, the weather. The usual suspects (sex, religion, politics) are usually taboo—see the information in Chapter 4: Making Friends. Small talk will abruptly end when it's time to "get down to business."

Step Into the Gap

What makes an American feel uncomfortable? As we've seen, it's silence! If there's a lull in the conversation, they feel compelled to jump in and fill it. One person picks up where the other left off—although to interrupt or talk over someone is considered rude. At the opposite extreme, being overly longwinded isn't appreciated, either. Congressional speakers, Oscar winners, and meeting participants alike are often given just thirty seconds to make their point before being unceremoniously cut off.

Manners

Manners are relaxed and informal but very much in evidence. "Please" is commonly used. "Yes, please" in response to being offered something might be replaced by "sure" or "okay," which may sound a little brusque to some ears. "Thank you" or "thanks" might be answered with a chipper "sure," "no problem," or slightly more formal "you're welcome." "Excuse me?" is the equivalent of the British "What did you say?" "Pardon?" or "Sorry?" And every stranger within earshot will "bless you" after you sneeze. (Or wish you "Gesundheit.") When Americans respond to a choice by saying "I don't care," it can sound, well, uncaring, but they usually mean "I don't mind." Text conversations may not end with a sign-off.

Political Correctness

This is one area where America is not quite so relaxed. Society and the workplace have to some extent been "sanitized" to ensure that no one is offended and everyone is included. Such gender-neutral terms as chairperson, firefighter, and mail carrier are commonplace. African-Americans, Native Americans, and LGBTQ folk are finally

Just Don't Call Me Late for Lunch

It's okay to refer to African-Americans as "Black." But don't use any other term, even if you hear Black people using it among themselves.

"Asian-American" means anyone whose origins are in Asia, including Southeast Asia and the Indian subcontinent. "Oriental" fell out of use years ago and is offensive.

"Hispanic" and "Latino" refer to people's ethnicity, not their race. Broadly, there's some Spanish-speaking folk in their background. The difference between the two terms can vary across the country.

"LGBTQ" is an acronym for Lesbian, Gay, Bisexual, Transgender, and either Queer or Questioning. "Gay" in this context means male homosexuals, although it's generally okay to use the term for both men and women. "Queer" is increasingly being used instead. You'll sometimes see LGBTQ2+ to include additional groups.

And for all the old-school fellas out there: *never* refer to women as "girls" in a business setting!

being addressed on their own terms. The result is an office communications culture that's relatively guarded. Visitors often note that Americans don't seem to "let their hair down" even at the office party. Remember, in the workplace, personal comments (even compliments) directed at a coworker with a different gender should be avoided, lest they be misconstrued as inappropriate or unwelcome—grounds for a sexual harassment charge. The "touchy-feely" days of the last century—the congratulatory pat on the back, the comforting arm round the shoulder—are long gone.

The Paper Trail

From the penning of the Constitution to today's litigious business environment, Americans trust only what's documented "on the record"—online or on paper. In such a large and diverse country, one can't assume that everyone's "on the same page" (in agreement) and people must "cover their tracks" (document everything), so "get it in writing."

BODY LANGUAGE

Handshakes are firm and accompanied by a smile and direct eye contact. This establishes credibility, conveying confidence and sincerity. In terms of a conversational "comfort zone," Americans normally prefer to keep at an arm's length distance, although they may briefly touch another's arm as a gesture of warmth or to emphasize a point. Of course, different habits apply if there's a current risk of infection. In this case, a recommended six-foot distance prevents any physical contact and will allow your interlocutor to feel comfortable.

In some cultures the degree of formality increases as one climbs the hierarchy. Not so in the USA where there is less "power-distance" between ranks. How do you detect "who's the boss" in a meeting? Not by seating arrangements or displays of deference, but by the relaxed yet authoritative style.

In terms of nonverbal gestures, it's difficult to generalize across regions without lapsing into stereotypes, but here goes. The Texans are renowned for their backslapping bonhomie, Midwesterners are more self-contained, Italian Americans gesticulate with their arms more than German Americans. High-fiving is commonplace among close friends, although a little gauche for the baby-boom generation. Covid-19 helped the fist bump (and the elbow bump) gain ground, and African-American culture has yielded the three-stage hand clasp—not to be attempted unless you know what you're doing.

Nonverbal gestures are always a cross-cultural minefield. For example, to indicate "good," an American might form thumb and forefinger into an "o" shape, a gesture that could be considered offensive elsewhere. Better to stick to the universal thumbs-up to express approval.

HUMOR

Whether born of brashness or insecurity, American humor isn't self-deprecating, individually or at the national level. Even professional comedians rarely tell jokes at their personal expense. Beyond this, the style of humor varies according to regional preferences and imported ethnic influences. American humor can range from cool, acerbic, cosmopolitan wit to the gentle, wry, nuanced storytelling of the heartland. As with so many aspects of American life,

Jewish people have made an inordinate contribution to the world of comedy and entertainment, from the Marx Brothers to Woody Allen and Larry David.

The preferred style may vary, but Americans like to surround themselves with humor. It's considered a national birthright to have a good time, and they'll readily reserve their sharpest put-downs for their neighboring state! Americans get their fun fix from TV sitcoms and comedy clubs, best-selling books, and online memes from digital sources like Reddit, The Onion, and Funny or Die.

The American home and office is festooned with cartoons on bulletin boards and joke-a-day calendars. Just remember, you're in the land of PC, so avoid telling jokes that may not land well. And avoid politics, too, unless you're sure of your audience.

THE NEWS MEDIA

In a 2021 survey, 86 percent of Americans said they get their news via the Internet, and this figure is only likely to have risen since. Television, meanwhile, came in second, being the go-to source for 68 percent of the population, while radio (50 percent) and print (32 percent) were clearly trailing. Of course, those sources overlap—cable news channels and magazines have their own Web sites, radio specials are downloadable, and every newspaper can deliver a morning roundup to your inbox in time for breakfast. American media is a mishmash, a vast global vat of words and images.

The good news is that the Fourth Estate—press and news media—operate under the First Amendment, that constitutional adjustment that granted freedom of speech and freedom of the press. The not-so-good news, perhaps, is that while the government can't interfere with the media, the owners of that media certainly can and do, staking out their position on the liberal-conservative spectrum. This echoes the present polarization of American politics, and many readers (or viewers or listeners) pick their sources to match their personal outlook, rarely hearing the "other side" of any issue.

The bottom line for the visitor is to know the reputation of their news source. Quality newspapers—and their Web sites—include the *New York Times*, *Washington Post*, *Boston Globe*, and *Los Angeles Times*. Additionally, there are news magazines such as *Time* or *Newsweek* for real news junkies, as well as a host of special interest publications like *Sports Illustrated* and *People*.

KEEPING IN TOUCH

Everybody Online

Nearly five billion people worldwide use the Internet. So, you probably know all about the leading apps that Americans use to keep in constant touch with friends, argue over the latest political outrage, and proudly showcase their own artistic and entertainment efforts.

Most Americans are online daily for an average of nearly eight hours a day. Like you, they interconnect with words, pictures, and videos—frequently in combination—through global channels such as Facebook, Instagram, Snapchat, TikTok, and WhatsApp. There's Twitter—dubbed "the world's town square"—for jokes and opinions, LinkedIn for jobs, and Tinder and Bumble among dozens of dating apps tailored to your flavor (and frequency) of "romance." And of course, there's YouTube, heading toward a billion videos, still dominated by content created by individual users, but—like many other platforms—also providing yet another pipeline for media companies, a soapbox for politicians and special interest groups, and a gateway for advertisers.

Wi-Fi hotspots are everywhere—not just in libraries, airports, hotel business centers, and Internet cafés, but in open public spaces, too, most of them available at no charge.

5G networks, which offer blazing speed connectivity, continue to spread across the USA. Currently, Verizon and T-Mobile are the wireless heavyweights, but AT&T and other carriers are catching up.

Telephones

With the spread of cell phones, public payphones are getting harder to find and have been largely converted to credit- or phone-card use only. At home, many Americans have ditched the landlines completely, or use a home phone service from the local cable company, packaged with broadband Internet access and a hundred or more channels of television.

Most people have a voicemail service and also "call waiting," so calls aren't missed and can be answered when convenient. But instant messaging has become the primary form of communication for social connections, as well as for business. Many would sooner type their messages these days than engage in a person-to-person phone call.

If your home mobile phone operates on the GSM frequency bands, then it should work in the USA, with either a GSM or CDMA carrier. Make sure it's unlocked, then purchase a SIM card, plug it in, and hope for the best! Or, buy a prepaid "burner" phone when you arrive. (You may also be able to download a burner phone app for your smartphone.) A dedicated phone store will be able to help you choose.

Calls from a hotel can be made collect, by credit card, or with a prepaid calling card, but the rates are exorbitant.

If you're calling the USA from overseas, dial your country's international access code (for example, 00 from the UK), the US country code (1), the three-digit area code (such as, 212 for New York), then the seven-digit phone number. Thus for New York 123 4567, you would dial, from the UK, 001 212 123 4567.

USEFUL NUMBERS

Information (Directory Assistance): 411

Emergencies: 911

Operator: 0

International Operator: 00

Mail

The postal service is reasonably reliable and inexpensive.
Post offices open generally from 9:00 a.m. to 5:00 p.m. To
avoid a lengthy wait, go at off-peak hours. Stamps can also
be bought at some supermarkets and even online. The
post office doesn't offer the wide range of goods (such as
stationery items) or services (such as bill paying) offered
in many other countries, although some packaging
supplies may be available.

Mail for travelers can be sent to any US post office. It
must be marked "General Delivery" and include the post
office zip (postal) code. To pick up a package, you'll
need to show a picture ID. Go to www.usps.com for
information on rates, zip codes, etc.

Private carriers such as FEDEX or United Parcel
Service (UPS) are expensive, but their home pick-up
service makes them a fast and convenient option.

CONCLUSION

It's getting harder than ever to pin down the "typical"
American. Perhaps that definition was already a moving
target before the ink on the Declaration of Independence
was dry. And yet there are still certain key, overarching
American values that infuse the spirit of every citizen—or
would-be citizen—whether he or she is a fresh immigrant
or a tenth-generation descendant of a Mayflower voyager.
We hope this book has captured that distinctive,
unmistakable national character: the drive for personal

advancement in a land that worships success, the expectation that any opinion can be freely expressed and any obstacle overcome, and an overwhelming sense of pride and patriotism in an America that—whether or not its faults are recognized or acknowledged—remains for its citizens the greatest nation on earth. As former president Bill Clinton said, "There is nothing wrong with America that cannot be cured by what is right with America."

Culture Smart! USA has set out a framework to enable you to appreciate this rich and fascinating country at many different levels. An understanding of the many cultures that make up America, and of the attitudes and behaviors you are likely to meet, will help you in business and in pleasure—and make you a better guest. Your visit will be all the more rewarding for it.

Now that you have a sense of what to expect, it's time to plan your visit. Where to start? How do you put your arms around a giant? Quite simply, you don't. You take it one state, one town, one main street, one serendipitous encounter at a time. By all means head for the iconic landmarks, the Grand Canyon, Niagara Falls, the Empire State Building, or the Alamo. But remember always that the most memorable and enriching experiences to be had in this great land are in the encounters with the people along the way.

USEFUL APPS

Travel and Transportation

Google Maps and **MapQuest** will get you where you want to go and show you what's around when you get there. **Waze** is an excellent navigation tool and includes up-to-date crowd-sourced information about traffic conditions. **Citymapper** is a popular route planning app that covers all modes of public transportation for dozens of US cities.

There are numerous hail-a-ride apps used across US cities. The most popular nationally include **Uber**, **Lyft**, **Curb**, and **Gett**. If you're driving, **Gasbuddy** can show you where to get the best price on gas nearby. The **Weather Channel** and **Dark Sky** will let you know what to expect from the elements.

AllTrails tells you about the best hiking, biking, and running trails in your area, including up-to-date information on trail quality and reviews from the hiking community. **Roadside America** is a humorous guide to more than 15,000 offbeat tourist attractions, museums, statues, art environments, and landmarks, with tips and stories. Maps and directions included.

Booking shows you what hotel rooms are nearby and what they're going to cost you. Both **Kayak** and **TripAdvisor** let you organize and track every aspect of your trip, with connections to hotels, airlines, car rentals, restaurants, etc. **FlightAware** lets you track airline flights, both internal and international, so you know about delays, cancellations, or gate changes.

Food, Shopping, and Entertainment

OpenTable shows you what's to eat nearby and then lets you book a table. Want to stay in instead? **Grubhub**, **Doordash**, and **UberEats** are a few of the many apps that'll bring local food to your door.

Groupon searches for discounts on everything you'll spend money on and **Yelp** is a great tool for finding restaurants, stores, and other services.

Headout shows you the top attractions, shows, tours, and experiences in popular cities like New York, Las Vegas, San Francisco, Los Angeles, Orlando, and more. **StubHub** puts you in touch with buyers and sellers of tickets for local concerts and sports events around the country. Made it to New York? Get advanced notice of the cut-price tickets for Broadway and off-Broadway shows that are on sale with **TKTS**.

When it comes to payment, bank and credit cards are widely accepted as is **Paypal**. Meanwhile, **Venmo** is great for person-to-person money transfers.

FURTHER READING

Althern, Gary, and Janet Bennett. *American Ways: A Cultural Guide to the United States of America*. Yarmouth, Maine: Intercultural Press, 2011.

Baker, Peter, and Susan Glasser. *The Divider: Trump in the White House, 2017-2021*. New York: Doubleday, 2022.

Bryson, Bill. *Made in America*. Great Britain: Martin Secker & Warburg Ltd., 1994.

——. *I'm A Stranger Here Myself: Notes on Returning to America After 20 Years Away*. New York: Broadway, 2000.

Froner, Eric. *The Story of American Freedom*. New York: W.W. Norton & Company, 1999.

Gwyne, S.C. *Empire of the Summer Moon: Quanah Parker and the Rise and Fall of the Comanches, the Most Powerful Indian Tribe in American History*. New York: Scribner, 2010.

Rankine, Claudia. *Citizen: An American Lyric*. Minneapolis: Graywolf Press, 2014.

Woodward, Colin. *American Character: A History of the Epic Struggle Between Individual Liberty and the Common Good*. London: Penguin Books, 2017.

Woodard, Colin. *American Nations: A History of the Eleven Rival Regional Cultures of North America*. London: Penguin Books, 2012.

PICTURE CREDITS

INDEX

9/11 attacks 49–51, 159

accommodation 156–7
address, forms of 63, 93, 183
affirmative action initiatives 69
Afghanistan, War in 49
African Americans 69, 82, 87, 187
age structure 11, 28, 102
air travel 152–3
Alaska 13, 26, 44
American Revolution 37–8
AmeriCorps 68
apartments 99
area 10, 13
arrival 147–8
art galleries 139–40
Articles of Confederation 37
Asian Americans 27, 87, 187
Atlanta, Battle of 42
ATMs 118, 159

Bar/Bat Mitzvahs 78
barbecue wars 127
bars 128–9
baseball 119–21, 123
basketball 121–2, 123
Biden, Joe 40, 52–3, 55
Bill of Rights 29–30
Bin Laden, Osama 51
birth/birthrate 27–8, 77, 102
Black Lives Matter 69
body language 188–9
Boston Tea Party 36
British 35, 36
Buddhism 76
bus travel 155
Bush, George H.W. 45, 49
Bush, George W. 34, 45, 49, 163
business briefing 163–79

"can-do" spirit 61–2

Capitol, attack on the 52
car rental 148, 150, 159
Carter, Jimmy 48–9
Catholicism 75
charity 68, 76
childcare 103, 111, 112
children 102, 103–5
Chinese community 87
Christianity 74–5, 86–7
Christmas 86, 94
church 8, 73–4
Civil Rights movement 48
Civil War 41–2
class, concepts of 63–4
climate 10, 14–15
climate change 50, 53, 67
Clinton, Bill 45, 49
Clinton, Hillary 45
cocktail parties 94–5, 179
coffee culture 128
Cold War 46–7
colonial rule 35–7
Columbus, Christopher 35
communications 181–94
Communism 47
competition 170–1
condo complexes 99
Confederate states 41–2
Congress 31
conservatism 66–7
Constitution 29–30, 38, 58, 70
control 62
conversation, topics of 91–2, 185
Covid-19 53–5, 103, 111, 164
Crazy Horse 41
credit/debit cards 118
Cuba 44, 47, 51
culture 132–43
currency 10
Custer, General 41
customs and traditions 73–87

daily life 111–13
death 77

Declaration of independence 37, 58
Democratic Party 32–3
dining etiquette 129–30
discrimination 43, 69, 178
diversity 69
divorce 101
DIY 100
dress code 95, 168–9
drink 128–9
driving 104–5, 148–52
Dutch Republic 37

eating out 125–32
economy 11, 163–5
education 104, 105–6, 107–11
egalitarianism 63–4
Electoral College 33, 34
electoral system 34, 63
Ellis Island (New York) 26
email 168
energy sources 62
entertaining, business 179
equality of opportunity 58–9, 69, 166
ethnic makeup 10, 26–9, 43
executive 30

families 101–3
fast food 127–8
festivals 79–87
film 140–1
First Communion 78
First World War 44
flag 13, 70–1
food 125–8
football 122–3
Ford, Henry 44–5
Founding Fathers 38, 64
Fourth of July 83
France 35, 37
Franklin, Benjamin 64
friendships 89–95

gaming 143
gated communities 99–100

GDP 163
gender equality 102–3
geography 13–14
gift-giving 94, 95
giving back 67–8
government 11, 29–34
grades 105–6
Great Depression 44–5
Great Lakes 13–14
greetings 93
Guam 13, 44
Gulf Stream 15
gun ownership/control 67, 160

Halloween 79, 84
handshakes 93
Harris, Kamala 53
Hawaii 13, 26, 44
health 50, 157–8, 164
higher education 109–11
Hinduism 76
Hispanic Americans 27, 187
history 34–53
home life 97–113
home, working from 167
Homestead Act (1862) 41
hospitality 89, 93–4
House of Representatives 31
housing 97–100
humor 189–90
Hurricane Katrina 49

ID 150, 153
ideal, American 57–8
immigration 9, 26–9, 43, 51, 69, 147
Independence Day 80, 83
Indian Removal Act (1830) 39
individualism 59–60, 66, 104
industrialization 43–4
insurance, health/travel 157–8
Internet 190, 191–2

introductions 92
invitations 90, 93–5
Iran hostage crisis 49
Iraq War 49
Islam 75–6, 87
isolationism, end of 44, 46

Jefferson, Thomas 38
Jehovah's Witnesses 76
Jews 75, 78, 87
Johnson, Lyndon 47
judiciary 31
Juneteenth 82

Kennedy, John F. 47, 67, 68
Kennedy, Robert 48
Khrushchev, Nikita 47
King, Martin Luther Jr. 48
Korean War 47

Labor Day 81
language 10, 181–3
legislature 31
leisure time 115–43
LGBTQ+ community 48, 186–7
life expectancy 11, 102
Lincoln, Abraham 42, 63
literature 138–9
Little Big Horn, Battle of 41
Louisiana Purchase 38

McCarthy, Joseph 47
mail services 194
management style 172
manifest destiny 38–41
manners 186
Mardi Gras 87
Mariana Islands, Northern 13
marijuana 132
marriage 77–8, 101
Marshall Plan 46
Martin Luther King Jr. Day 82
Mayflower 35
media 11, 190–1

meetings 174–5
Memorial Day 81
meritocracy 58, 170
Mexico/Mexicans 51, 53, 87
Middle Atlantic 17–19
middle class 64
Midwest 19–20
Missouri–Mississippi River system 14
money 118
Monroe, James 44
Moon landings 48, 61
morality 66–7
Mormons 76
multiculturalism 29, 69, 77
museums 139–40
music 135–8
musical theater 133–4

national anthem 70, 71
Native Americans 14, 26, 38–41
natural resources 11
negotiations 176–7
networking 92, 172
New Age practices 77
New Deal 45
New England 16–17
newspapers 11, 190, 191
Nixon, Richard 48
nuclear war 46, 47

Obama, Barack 49–51, 52, 53, 163, 164
opening hours 113
outsourcing 165, 166
overseas travel 91, 116, 146

Panama Canal 44
paper trail 168, 188
Paris Climate Agreement 50, 53
Paris, Treaty of 37
patriotism 70–1
Peace Corps 68
people 26–9
personal space 110–11

Plymouth Colony 35–6
politeness 89
political correctness 186–8
politics 32–3, 63, 66, 91–2
population 10
populism 63
potluck dinners 94
poverty 8, 60
presentations 175–6
presidency 30, 34
President's Day 81
Pride parades 87
Prom Night 78
Protestantism 74–5
public (federal) holidays 79–82
public transportation 155–6
Puerto Rico 13, 44
Puritans 35–6, 66

questions, personal 91
Quinceaneros 78

radio 11, 142–3, 190
railroads 43, 154–5
rainfall 15
Raleigh, Walter 35
Reagan, Ronald 49, 66
recession (2009) 163
regions 15–26
religion 11, 58, 66, 73–7, 92
Republican Party 32–3, 66
restaurants 94, 125–8
restrooms 157
rites of passage 77–8
road travel 148–52
Roosevelt, Eleanor 45
Roosevelt, Franklin Delano 45
Roosevelt, Theodore 45

safety 158–60
St. Patrick's Day 80–1
Samoa, American 13
Saratoga, Battle of 37
schools 105, 106, 107–9

Second World War 46
sects, religious 76
self-promotion 170–1
self-reliance 60–1, 66, 104
Senate 31
Seven Years' War 36
Seventh Day Adventists 76
shopping 113, 116–18
skyscrapers 43–4
slavery 41–2, 43
small talk 185
smoking 131–2
soccer 124
social media 105, 192
social status 63–4
South 24–5
Southwest 22–4
Spain 35, 37
Spanish–American War 44
speed limits 151
sport 118–24, 185
state governments 31–2
streaming 11, 142–3
suburbs 99
Supreme Court 30, 31, 73

taboo subjects 91–2, 185
taxis 156
tea 128
teamwork 173–4
telephones 11, 113, 168, 192–3
television 11, 115, 141–2, 190
temperatures 14–15
terrain 10, 13–14
territories and dependencies 13
terrorism 49, 50, 159
text-based communication 168
Thanksgiving 79, 80, 84–6, 94
theater 133–4
time, attitude towards 62, 65
time zones 8, 11
tipping 131

titles 93, 183
Trail of Tears 39
travel 145–57
Trump, Donald 34, 45, 51–2, 54, 66, 164

Ukraine, War in 53, 165
Union states 41–2
urbanization 98

vacations 65, 116, 146
vaccinations 54–5
Valentine's Day 79, 82–3
values and attitudes 57–71
Veteran's Day 81
Vietnam War 47–8
Vikings 34
Virgin Islands, US 13
volunteering 68

Washington, George 38, 63
Watergate scandal 48
wealth 8, 163
weather, extreme 14–15, 160–1
weddings 77–8
West 21–2
wildfires 15, 161
wildlife 161
Wilson, Woodrow 44
women
  in business 178–9
  working 111–12
work ethic 64–5, 108
working environment 165–71
working hours 65, 166

Yorktown, Siege of 37

Zangwill, Israel 28, 29